WILLIAM BLAKE

WILLIAM BLAKE

Frontispiece

WILLIAM BLAKE

BY

BASIL DE SELINCOURT

AUTHOR OF "GIOTTO"

NEW YORK
COOPER SQUARE PUBLISHERS, INC.
1971

Originally Published 1909
Published 1971 by Cooper Square Publishers, Inc.
59 Fourth Avenue, New York, N. Y. 10003
International Standard Book No. 0-8154-0389-5
Library of Congress Catalog Card No. 72-162018

Printed in the United States of America

PREFACE

THE obligations I have incurred in the process of forming my estimate of Blake and preparing materials for this monograph are more numerous than I can name. In the first place, my friend Mrs. Sturge Henderson has given me the benefit of a rare critical ability and advanced my work in all its stages by her encouragement and advice. Then the exhibition of Blake's work, held at the Carfax Gallery in 1906, gave me exceptional facilities for a collective study of his masterpieces, and by the hospitable kindness of the proprietors I was enabled to avail myself of these in a singular degree. Mr. More Adey furthered my studies by placing his wide and accurate knowledge of Blake's technical processes completely at my disposal, and did me most generous service in assisting me to procure adequate illustration for the work. Mr. A. G. B. Russell very genially welcomed me as collaborator in a field where collaborators cannot be wanted, and it was through his courtesy that I was able to enrich my pages with four reproductions from Captain Archibald Stirling's superb coloured copy of the *Jerusalem* ; to Captain Stirling also my warm thanks are due. Mr. W. Graham Robertson has permitted me to publish reproductions of seven of the drawings in his unique collection, and I could gladly have leaned more upon his liberality than I have, but that other claimants had forestalled me. Mr. George Macmillan and Sir Charles Dilke have also kindly allowed me to reproduce works in their possession ; and I have to thank the authorities at the Fitzwilliam Museum at Cambridge for a similar permission. I am also indebted to Professor Tylor, and to Messrs. W. Bateson, A. M. S. Methuen, and Bowes Morrell, for lending to me or otherwise allowing me to inspect the books and pictures in their possession. The authorities at the South Kensington and at the British Museum have met my demands with their usual long-suffering kindness ; and I must not forget the advantage I received from the presence of a Blake specialist in the Print Room.

The inception of the work was due to the enthusiasm of a friend, who will, I fear, view only with regret my qualified devotion to my subject.

KINGHAM, 1909.

CONTENTS

ILLUSTRATIONS

ix   *b*

CHAPTER I

BLAKE'S LIFE

THE history of Blake's life has been so often written that it would waste ink and paper to write it over again. Thanks to researches undertaken by Mr. Arthur Symons, we know now exactly where each member of Blake's family was christened and where buried, with the registered number and the cost of their graves. We know also that Blake was not the son of an Irish runaway who had changed his name. Who but an Irishman could have supposed he was so? The most remarkable fact about Blake is the stability of his character : that a man so impressionable and so hot-headed never left his moorings. Undoubtedly they were both deep and strong. Internal evidence is all in favour of his having come of a settled orderly stock, and, taken with this, the external evidence produced by Mr. Symons suffices to put Messrs. Ellis and Yeats's theory finally out of count. Blake was the son of a small hosier who lived in Broad Street, Golden Square,

a quarter of London where there had been Blakes
settled all through the eighteenth century.   But
Blake's father, besides being a hosier, was one of the
first members of the still surviving sect of Sweden-
borgians.   Thus the spirit of Nonconformity ran in
Blake's veins from the first.   He lived in a household
where the Bible was read with all the constancy and
fervour which naturally arise when new interpretations
are to be imposed on a familiar text.   This provides the
determinant feature of his life.   He was an active Non-
conformist to the end.   The " Dissidence of Dissent "
seldom attracted a more whole-hearted worshipper.
Only his artistic preoccupations prevented him from
becoming the apostle of a crusade against custom.

As to his life itself, the main outlines of it are sufficiently well known.   Blake's character is so absorbing
that there is a temptation to regard his circumstances
as of more interest than they are.   The fact is that they
merit the epithet which has been applied to them by
Blake's most recent critic and eulogist in France.
They were *banal*.   It comes somewhat as a shock to
the English reader to receive this information, but the
truth, having been told, must be admitted.   A com-
plaint is sometimes made, that we know too little of
Blake's outward affairs.   This is a mistake.   The
representative facts are before us : we know enough to

be sure that the inward and outward were, throughout his life, related negatively. Blake's circumstances tell us what he was not; it is to his activity as an artist and a thinker that we must turn if we wish to discover what he was.

The natural stability of temperament that underlay Blake's tempestuous exterior was doubtless fostered and maintained by his discipline and practice as an engraver. His unusual gifts were early recognised by his parents. At ten years old he attended a good drawing school and learned to copy from the antique; at fourteen he was apprenticed to the well-known engraver Basire. Basire was clearly a man of strong character; of all who came into direct touch with Blake, none influenced him more powerfully. Basire's methods were the contrary of those to which Blake would naturally have been attracted. He pursued definiteness and precision at the expense of other qualities hardly less essential to the arts. But his sound craftsmanship left an ineffaceable impression on Blake's mind, and he was perhaps the only one of Blake's contemporaries for whom he maintained an unwavering respect. Basire, moreover, had wit to perceive his pupil's singular capabilities. It cannot have been mere chance that sent Blake, still an apprentice, to make copies for his master of the tombs of the Kings and other Gothic monuments preserved in the Abbey and in all the ancient churches of London.[1] This task was decisive in its effect upon Blake's mental development. The turn of mind which led him to revert in literature to the Elizabethans was already pronounced. His prolonged study of Gothic form, carried on during the most impressionable years of his life, nourished all the romantic instincts by which he was allied with Shakespeare and with Fletcher, and gave him a permanent bias in his method of presenting them. In his most perfect work he is almost always breathing again the atmosphere with which these years made him familiar. And who can doubt it was because the church was so long his studio that subjects such as Time or Death or Eternity—subjects hardly calculated in themselves to inspire a painter's imagination—continued through life to exercise the strongest fascination over his mind? Few of his inventions are more beautiful and none nearer to what is most intimate and most individual in the inventor than that which shows the *Counsellor, King, Warrior, Mother and Child, in the Tomb.*

[1] The Society of Antiquaries is still in possession of some half-dozen drawings, most of them signed by Basire, but presumably his pupil's work. The most interesting is that of the north front of King Sebert's tomb. In the expression given to the figures and in his delight in all the details of the ornament, the artist shows himself essentially Gothic at heart.

THE DOOR OF DEATH
BRITISH MUSEUM

To face p. 4

With his apprenticeship to Basire Blake's education both began and ended; his faults all his life through are essentially the faults of an uneducated man. His intellectual absolutism and the reckless consistency of his mental outlook are traits which history cannot often have paralleled. He was confirmed in them by a natural antipathy to the dominant ideas of his age. Wherever facts might have wrung a concession from him, he was able, by unconscious jugglery, to see them as the prejudices of his contemporaries; and he exalted his own prejudices, self-absorption and radical unteachableness to a level with his inspiration. He read widely, but never showed the least faculty, in literature any more than in life, of entering into any other attitude of mind than that which was native to him; and though it was a part of his theory that truth must appear different to different minds, his practice amounted to a dogmatic denial of the existence of more than one way of approaching it. Nothing more clearly indicates this than his horror of the idea of education itself.

Thank heaven [he writes] I never was sent to school
To be flogg'd into following the style of a fool.

He conceived education, apparently, as a purely mechanical process, a stocking of the mind with ready-made ideas. He had a quite clear and consistent view on this point from the time when he wrote his lovely song *The Schooolboy* to the time when he told Crabb Robinson "There is no use in education; I hold it wrong." He was its declared enemy; as he was the enemy of everything that appeared to encroach on the domain of spontaneous development. But his theory was falsified in his life. In poetry, where he has no teacher, Blake drifts rapidly into a sea of shapeless vapours; in painting, though his ideas grow more and more peculiar, he gains rather than loses in the power to render them characteristically.

Marriage, with the qualities of constraint and continuity which are inseparable from it, is sometimes a means of opening the mind to truths—in particular to truths of temperament—which the unattached may readily succeed in evading. But Blake in whatever circumstances he had been placed would probably have proved unsusceptible of this kind of discipline. In their early married days his wife had a dispute with her brother-in-law Robert who was then sharing their home. "Kneel down and beg Robert's pardon directly," Blake said to her, "or you never see my face again." Catherine obeyed, Robert at once admitting that the wrong had been on his side not hers. Blake's method and his wife's submission to it indicate clearly the attitude which both found it natural he should take up. There was only one kind of marriage contract to which Blake could really have subscribed. He owed its fulfilment to the chance that brought him a wife who cared for him enough to be willing to lose her personality in his. Catherine became in fact an ideal second self, neither too insignificant nor too significant. In this way, while securing him wonderful freedom for the development and expression of his ideas, she unconsciously fostered some of the less desirable elements in her husband's mystical scheme. Needless to say, this scheme was built out of his experience; perhaps no more need be added than that, if Blake's wife had been richer in independence of character, the "female" could hardly have been disposed of in it after a manner so convenient to the "male." Blake, on his side, knew how to win and how to maintain her touching devotion and fidelity.

A word must be said of Blake's appearance and physique. Various well-known portraits suffice to show how remarkable it was. That by Phillips enforces the rhetorical side of Blake's inspiration rather uncomfortably. Linnell's miniature embodies something at once sweeter and more deeply characteristic, showing in the head a wonderful monument of vigorous yet crystallised intellect. In an ambitious "fresco" which represented

the last battle of King Arthur and the three Britons
who escaped therefrom—types of " the beautifullest, the
strongest and the ugliest" man respectively—Blake made
the type of the strongest man conformable to his own.
The picture is, unfortunately, missing, and those who
wish to discover Blake in his designs must examine his
drawings of " Los." But interesting remarks about the
strongest man are to be read in the *Descriptive Catalogue*. He represents the " human sublime," and is " a
receptacle of wisdom ; " " his features and limbs do not
spindle out into length without strength, nor are they
too large and unwieldy for his brain and bosom.
Strength consists in accumulation of power to the
principal seat, and from thence a regular gradation and
subordination. The strong man acts from conscious
superiority, and marches on in fearless dependence on
the divine decrees, raging with the inspirations of a prophetic mind." Blake was, as a matter of fact, short of
stature and extremely powerfully built. In their early
married days, he and his wife would walk forty miles
at a stretch, he no doubt stimulating her energy out of
the superabundance of his own. " Once," Gilchrist
narrates, " a young artist called and complained of being
very ill; what was he to do ? ' Oh,' said Blake, ' I
never stop for anything ; I work on whether ill or not.' "
Our frontispiece shows well the towering forehead,

and splendid concentration of mien in mouth and
brow, which made Blake wherever he went a man of
mark. The paler effigy on the same sheet is by Mrs.
Blake, notable only for the hair, which is said to have
stood up in Blake's youth like flames around his head.
He was fully conscious of his peculiarities of feature,
and took no small pleasure in them. Having a snub
nose, he believed it an essential part of Christianity
to have one; when Crabb Robinson asked him " what
affinity he supposed there was between the *genius* that
inspired Socrates and his own *spirits?*" he replied
" the same as in our countenances."

The chief events of Blake's early life were the composing and illustrating of his poetical sketches and
songs, and all those fresh raptures and enthusiasms of
youth without which he never could have conceived
them. But his experience already had two sides.
His introduction to the Mathews, his acceptance of
the generous offer which led to the publication, or at
least to the printing, of his first volume of verse, his
early withdrawal from their polite and hospitable
circle, and the reflections on the society he found
there which he allows himself in the doggerel prose of
his *Island in the Moon,* place certain limitations of his
character before us with painful clearness. We receive
an unpleasant shock in lighting upon some jewel from

the *Songs of Innocence* half buried in, this morass of
scurrilous abuse and plebeian coarseness, where,
with all its forced merriment, there is never the least
trace of wit. Nor is it useful to blind our eyes to
Blake's responsibility for what he wrote. It expressed
one aspect of his character. His passionate pursuit
of freedom, his fearless identification of himself with
the revolutionary party in England and in France,
his enthusiastic championship of the Americans in
their struggle for independence, were not the outcome
of any enlarged practice of human sympathy; they
merely witnessed a blind impulsive adhesion to an
abstract principle which, on his first entry into a
drawing-room, Blake showed himself unable to apply.
Throughout life he remained supremely egotistical,
with an egotism only the more complete that he was
unconscious of it. Courteous, compassionate, generous,
large-minded, he was never able to enter into the
natural intercourse of equality as between man and
man. He appears to have alternated in his demeanour
between a marked and deferential amenity and a
passionate self-assertiveness, the amenity being often
little more than a mask, assumed by pride for the
concealment of an almost rancorous distaste. When
Reynolds told him to correct his drawing, Blake
probably responded with one of his sweetest smiles.

But the memory of the insult was a red rag to him all the rest of his days.

After completing his apprenticeship, Blake took a partner and set up in business as an engraver on his own account: in this he failed: no doubt it was an exacting enterprise. Later he was so far successful in forming connections as a drawing-master that he was recommended for appointment to the King's household. He felt obliged to decline this honour, and, in order to be able to do so graciously, withdrew from all his other engagements as a teacher. Nothing is known of the process by which Blake reached this pinnacle of worldly prosperity. His withdrawal from it was effected in characteristic style. The incident belongs to the period of his residence in Hercules Buildings, Lambeth, a period of extraordinary productiveness both in poetry, prophecy, and design. No evidence is wanting to show that Blake's spiritual avocations did not in themselves unfit him for the humdrum of practical affairs. The extreme poverty in which the best part of his life was passed fell upon him not from any want of aptitude or application—he was a man of immense energy and never cared for anything more than for his work—but because he no sooner found himself on the road to success than he was afraid of it.

The central episode of Blake's career is his visit to Felpham, and it is of interest that just before setting out he viewed his life in retrospect and noted what he considered the principal influences which had moulded it.

TO MY DEAREST FRIEND, JOHN FLAXMAN, THESE LINES:

I bless thee, O Father of Heaven and Earth, that ever I
    saw Flaxman's face.
Angels stand round my spirit in Heaven, the blessed of
    Heaven are my friends upon earth.
When Flaxman was taken to Italy, Fuseli was given to me
    for a season,
And now Flaxman has given me Hayley, his friend, to be
    mine, such my lot upon earth.
Now my lot in the Heavens is this; Milton lov'd me in
    childhood and show'd me his face.
Ezra came with Isaiah the prophet, but Shakespeare in
    riper years gave me his hand.
Paracelsus and Behmen appeared to me, terrors appeared
    in the Heavens above,
And in Hell beneath, and a mighty and awful change
    threatened the earth.
The American war began. All its dark horrors passed
    before my face
Across the Atlantic to France. Then the French Revolu-
    tion commenced in thick clouds,

And my Angels have told me that seeing such visions I
    could not subsist on the earth,
But by my conjunction with Flaxman, who knows to for-
    give nervous fear.

These lines illustrate well the soaring vehemency of
Blake's affection and gratitude at times when such
feelings were uppermost in his mind ; and the account
of his lot in the heavens is full of illumination. The
list of influences is far from complete. Some of the
most fundamental are, as naturally they would be,
presupposed ; yet as a whole it is highly representative.
Blake caught much of his manner from inferior models,
not excluding Ossian ; but Milton, Shakespeare, Behmen, Isaiah, may be taken as typical of the influences
which worked immediately upon him ; and the events
of his life, up to the time of his unhappy flight to
Felpham, were the world-moving events in which
Wordsworth and Coleridge also found their inspiration.
He himself began a poem on the Revolution, which was
to comprise seven books, the first being published for
him anonymously by Johnson in 1791. Nothing is
known about its contents. A perfervid revolutionist
in theory, and one who had been ready in his early
years for the sake of his principles to expose himself to
danger in the streets of London, he soon lost sympathy
with the resort to physical violence. The regions of

the spirit gave scope for a violence so much more
protracted and more intense. Moreover, the war and
the revolution, even while they went on, were much
less facts to him than types of a recurrent spiritual
manifestation. He regarded the whole of history, not
as a process of events in time, but as the perpetual re-
enactment of a truth which every man might find
written for himself in the conditions of his individual
life. The result of such an outlook was rather the
narrowing of the world to the scale of the individual
than the enlargement of the individual to more vital
sympathy with the world. Thus the great events of
which he was a witness seemed literally to have affected
him in the manner which in these lines he attributes
to them metaphorically; they were like some stupen-
dous display of electric or volcanic phenomena, indu-
cing terror and stirring life to its deeps, yet with
nothing in them which could make direct appeal to
the human heart or tend to any kind of reasonable
adaptation of the private to the universal need. Nor
is there any evidence that Blake continued to follow
the course of events when they ceased to force themselves upon his notice. The war and the revolution
were visions while they lasted and they remained with
him as visions all his life. They intensified his sense
of the internal spiritual struggle which was, in his

view, the essence of the life of the individual, magni-
fying, so to speak, enormously the stature of the
giants by whom he pictured this struggle carried on.
But they did nothing to bring him more closely into
touch with the world of flesh and blood where they
were enacted: on the contrary, they drove him more
deeply upon himself.

The struggle between the two sides of Blake's
nature comes out with remarkable completeness in
his intercourse with Hayley. It seems a pity, because
Hayley was a person of only momentary significance, to deface his memory more than is needful
in order to emphasise—a thing in itself so obvious—
the contrast between his character, not to say his gifts,
and Blake's. Hayley's conduct of the affair was
dignified and in keeping with his position. Blake's
was not. Of course it was because Blake was greater
that he had the harder task. Hayley played upon
Blake's sensitiveness without the least consciousness of
what he was about. Blake read Homer with his
patron, painted miniatures, engraved tombstones, drew
pictures of animals to illustrate ballads in the *eau-sucré*
style; and all the time, under his mask of civility,
plunged like a harpooned leviathan, scattering seas of
foam and blood. The performance was not to his
credit, and his attempt to read a deep spiritual signifi-

cance into it adds an element of the ridiculous to its futility. It is pathetic to see a fish flopping on dry land; but who would attend to the theory of the proceedings it might devise after being put back into the water?

Blake's stay at Felpham, and the capital he made out of it—nothing less than a history of " the spiritual acts of his three years slumber upon the banks of Ocean," written at intervals under inspiration and so completed into a poem, which he believed the grandest this world contains—reveal a condition of mental isolation in him so startling that the mind almost refuses to take it in. The world he inhabited was a world which he had created for himself out of his thoughts and his dreams and his pure idealistic passion, centred always upon its vivid, yet confined, conception of spiritual life. It was because his world was in this sense all his own that the least incursion into it by another, whether by conflict of wills, or by the expression of so much as a difference of opinion, affected him as if it were an act of trespass prompted by malice. As Flaxman, in a letter to Hayley, well expressed it: " Blake's irritability, as well as the association and arrangement of his ideas, do not seem likely to be soothed or more advantageously disposed by any power inferior to that by which man is originally endowed with his faculties." At Felpham

too, he was more sensitive than at any time before or
afterwards. He had been born and had lived all his
life in London; and he was far too childlike to understand and allow for the effects of solitude and monotony
upon nerves and brain. Whatever happened had for
him all the significance which at the moment it appeared to have. Thus his life in the quiet cottage
became a series of portentous revolutions; the veins
stood out upon his forehead at the recollection of what
he had passed through. How different the hopes in
which he had set out, when the vision of Felpham was
as Jacob's vision, with a ladder to heaven and angels
ascending and descending between heaven and earth,
when "the sweet air and the voices of winds, trees, and
birds, and the odours of the happy ground, make it a
dwelling for immortals." "Work will go on here with
God-speed. A roller and two harrows" (sacred symbols) "lie before my window. I met a plough on my
first going out at my gate the first morning after my
arrival, and the plough-boy said to the ploughman,
'Father, the gate is open.'"

From first to last the associations of the pastoral
life were among the deepest springs of Blake's inspiration. So tender is his intimacy with the countryside
in all its broader aspects that, reading his songs, one
might easily forget his London origin. The sympathy

B

and intuitive understanding he betrays in his exquisite *Auguries of Innocence* are something unique in kind. Yet there is no incident recorded to show that he ever came outwardly into touch with animals or knew their ways. If they were nearer to him than men were, it was, perhaps, because they had no private opinions. Blake pleads their cause with delicatest discernment, and he, who heralded a new poetry and a new painting, or rather testified afresh to the old which is for ever new, was herald in this also of the gentler humanity which is still only beginning to find general voice. The London of his day was, of course, very different from ours, and, as a boy, he was able to walk through the lovely orchards and hayfields of Camberwell, and to find angels there. But if there are any who still suppose that the true poet of shepherds must be a shepherd himself, Blake's pastoral poems and designs will not support them. He touched perfection here. But the vision was intense partly because the object was unfamiliar. The effect of the country, when he found himself alone in it, was deadening. Something, of course, must be allowed for the excessive stimulus it offered to his artistic sense, no doubt producing subsequent reaction. But the fact remains that his habits were essentially the habits of a Londoner, and in all the externals of his life, his later life particularly,

Why should the mistress of the vales of Har, utter a sigh.

She ceas'd & smild in tears, then sat down in her silver shrine.

Thel answerd. O thou little virgin of the peaceful valley.
Giving to those that cannot crave, the voiceless, the o'ertired
Thy breath doth nourish the innocent lamb, he smells thy milky garments,
He crops thy flowers, while thou sittest smiling in his face,
Wiping his mild and meekin mouth from all contagious taints.
Thy wine doth purify the golden honey, thy perfume,
Which thou dost scatter on every little blade of grass that springs,
Revives the milked cow, & tames the fire-breathing steed.
But Thel is like a faint cloud kindled at the rising sun:
I vanish from my pearly throne, and who shall find my place.

Queen of the vales the Lilly answerd, ask the tender cloud,
And it shall tell thee why it glitters in the morning sky.
And why it scatters its bright beauty thro' the humid air.
Descend O little cloud & hover before the eyes of Thel.

The Cloud descended, and the Lilly bowd her modest head:
And went to mind her numerous charge among the verdant grass.

THEL AND THE LILY

BRITISH MUSEUM

To face p. 18

he might have been admirably fitted to one of Charles
Dickens's canvasses. It is said that for years together
he never left his rooms, except to fetch his daily pint
of porter from a neighbouring public house; and then
there is the charming story which Gilchrist tells, how a
nobleman once sent Blake some spirit distilled from
walnuts for artistic uses, which Blake, on tasting,
found so good that he continued, absent-mindedly,
to apply it to his lips instead of to his canvas until
there was no more left. One can see the far-away
expression of his eye as the aroma mingled with his
meditations.

After his return from Felpham he settled for nearly
twenty years in lodgings in South Molton Street,
Lambeth, and here his circumstances grew more and
more straitened, his material need adding, as was
natural, a new bitterness to his natural perversity of
bearing towards friends and employers. It was here
that Cromek, the engraver and publisher, found him
living with his wife on half a guinea a week. Like
Hayley, Cromek has been too much abused. After all,
he had the sense to recognise the value of Blake's designs,
and the illustrations to Blair's *Grave*, which he was the
means of putting before the world, were for a long
time Blake's only title to fame. Undoubtedly, he was
an unpleasant man, and the letter he has left behind

him shows that he could be not only careless but vulgar
in his bearing towards Blake's sensitiveness and pride.
But it is impossible to determine the true merits of
their quarrel. Cromek would certainly have lied when
convenient; Blake, with perfect rectitude of intention,
could never be trusted to know the difference between
what was false and what was true. Thus the facts are
quite unascertainable. However, we know that Blake
had twenty guineas for his designs and the best introduction to the wider public life ever offered him. It
was not Cromek's fault that Blake had not the
character or temperament which might have enabled
him to make the wide circulation of the *Grave* a
stepping-stone to better things. Blake saw nothing
but insult and loss in the entire transaction; and the
degree of recognition he gained by it served only to
convince him how much more was his due. He came
to believe that there was a conspiracy to obscure him,
and launched out into extravagant and futile self-
praise. He even convinced himself that it was his
duty to the public to inform all and sundry that he
was one of the great artists of the world, and to sub-
stantiate the claim embarked on several enterprises—
the engraving of his *Canterbury Pilgrims* among them
—which were quite beyond his means. The result is
that for something near ten years he sinks into an

almost unrelieved obscurity, broken, if at all, by revelations which fill the eyes with tears. One of his note-
books, the same, I think, as that in which the fiery
lines of his *Everlasting Gospel* were jotted down, has
an entry, dated with the day and the hour, of the
single word "Despair." Blake was intensely proud
and self-assured ; the anguish of heart needed to
wring such a confession from him must be passed
silently by.

His life must have been a tragedy, but for the happy
chance which towards the end brought him, in John
Linnell, a friend able to give him a discerning sympathy, to pay him the homage he needed and deserved,
and to be a buffer between him and the outside world,
mitigating its jars and translating them into a language which he could understand. Thus the menace
of tragedy is resolved ; the last scene is romantic,
almost pastoral, and closes in a clear evening radiance.
The figure of Blake emerges from affliction, and, like
the summer sun, surrounds itself with a perfect tranquillity and tenderness as it comes near the fulfilment
of its course. It is in these last years, more than at
any other period of his life, that Blake's spiritual
stature is most clearly manifested. We recognise that
the fret and fever of earlier times was incidental ; that
the troubles, however agitating, had been upon the

surface, and that below there had always remained still waters, deep and undisturbed. The coterie of young artists, Palmer, Richmond, Calvert, who learned at this time to look to Blake as to their leader, prove how unique a combination of enthusiasm, reverence, and love he inspired both by his works and by the fragrant simplicity and content in which his days were passed. It is only with this vision before us—as we see him patiently working at the great series of engravings that have secured him immortality—that we can put the violence, the vituperations, the self-assertion of his maturity into their relative place. For, after all, Blake was something very like, something, indeed, almost as great as he pretended to be. The calm light, the noble achievement of his parting years take us back to the budding joys, the sacred ecstasies, the unexampled promise, of his youth and opening manhood. And all his life through we find what is most characteristic of him in the occasionally recorded incident showing that his childlike trust in goodness, his spontaneous aspiration after beauty, his impassioned reverence and awe before the mystery of the spirit of life, were with him day by day and hour by hour. These are the stuff of which great art is made; and Blake, though too much let and hindered to rise to a place among the greatest, completely lacking in

the breadth and sanity of outlook which endow a man's
work with temperance, humility, and graciousness, and
teach him the virtue of speaking in such tones as his
fellows can enjoy and understand, yet often has been
and perhaps always will be compared, and compared
justly, with men who, like Giotto, Angelico, or even
Michael Angelo, have seen deepest the nature of the
divine humanity and have embodied what they saw.
Blake suffered as an artist from having no consistency
of aim ; he theorised perpetually, but never came to a
clear understanding with himself. And even if in his
art he had known what course he was steering, his
philosophy must have turned the boat awry. His
method is now Gothic, now Oriental, now pseudo-
Renaissance ; he takes us at one time to Florence, at
another to Siena, or to Nuremburg ; and finding
wherever we go with him the same stamp of individuality upon his work, we are tempted, at last, to
look for it in that want of perfect fulfilment which
almost everywhere accompanies him. Never, indeed,
was there an artist more baffling, more unseizable. To
discover his greatness we must turn rather to the
tenderness, the intimacy, the intensity with which he
sees than to the substance of his vision or to the
ordering and development of the means by which he
reveals it. After his first outburst of lyric ecstasy it is

for the most part only in an occasional phrase, slipping
out unawares — phrases like his "tent of elegant
beauty," or of honeysuckle, when he describes how
" the flaunting beauty revels along upon the wind "—
that we catch the quality of his poetic insight, or
realise what a master of language he might have been.
With further qualification the same is true of the
designs. His greatness is generally in the parts, in the
breath or flow of a feeling too fierce or too delicate to
be consciously worked out; in all that is indeliberate,
unconscious, fragmentary. He has moments of exquisite
perception, movements unfathomable in their origin,
tremendous in their aim, and sometimes awful as they
proceed to its fulfilment. But the sublimest of his
conceptions are often marred by evidences of a strained
imagination and fail of their effect. Whatever the
vein of his activity, he "exists and exults in immortal
thoughts," and when, in controversy with a patron, he
"names Moses, Solomon, Æsop, Homer, Plato," as men
to whom he naturally turns as supporters, our sense of
his arrogance cannot withhold from him an amused
smile of assent. There is, so to speak, an aristocracy
of intuition, of men who, whether or no amplified
correspondingly in the gifts and graces of common life,
move in a closer relation than their fellows to the
source from which our variable life proceeds. Of these

Blake is emphatically one ; this it is that turns all his
failures into a kind of successes, and gives even to the
most extravagant of his perversities and the most mis-
leading of his falsehoods something of the healing and
inspiring influence of truth.

CHAPTER II

BLAKE'S SECRET

BEFORE Blake can be appreciated truly for what he is, the lumber heaped around him by a lifeless age, or rather by himself in his reaction against its lifelessness, must be cleared relentlessly away. This task has been made the more necessary because the current of Blake criticism in recent years has been flowing in another direction. The fact that he was once misunderstood, mistaken for a mere raver, has induced minds naturally sympathetic with the general tenor of his life and thought to think of it as far more unimpeded in its inner development and its artistic expression than it actually was. Blake himself regarded his spiritual life as an internecine conflict. " I have travelled," he writes, " through perils and darkness not unlike a champion." " Nothing can withstand the fury of my course among the stars of God and in the abysses of the accuser." And expressions like these—endorsed as they are by the prevailing tone of

Awake! Awake Jerusalem! O lovely Emanation of Albion
Awake and overspread all Nations as in Ancient Time
For lo! the Night of Death is past and the Eternal Day
Appears upon our Hills: Awake Jerusalem, and come away

So spake the Vision of Albion & in him so spake in my hearing
The Universal Father Then Albion stretchd his hand into Infinitude.
And took his Bow. Fourfold the Vision for bright beaming Urizen
Layd his hand on the South & took a breathing Bow of carved Gold
Luvah his mand stretchd to the East & bore a Silver Bow bright shining
Tharmas Westward a Bow of Brass pure flaming richly wrought
Urthona Northward in thick storms a Bow of Iron terrible thundering
And the Bow is a Male & Female & the Quiver of the Arrows of Love.
Are the Children of this Bow; a Bow of Mercy & Loving kindness; laying
Open the hidden Heart in Wars of mutual Benevolence Wars of Love
And the Lord of Man grasped firm between the Male & Female Loves
And he Clothed himself in Bow & Arrows in awful state Fourfold
in the midst of his Twenty-eight Cities each with his Bow breathing

"THE FURY OF MY COURSE AMONG THE STARS"

BRITISH MUSEUM

To face p. 26

his writing in the *Milton* and *Jerusalem*—give undoubtedly a truer view of his mind when its strength
was at the highest than is to be gleaned from the more
familiar picture presented to us in Crabb Robinson's
reminiscences, where the last mild years of reconciliation are reflected; a reconciliation, more with
himself than with the world—the time when, since
his own paradoxes had ceased to startle him, he could
return to the unclouded fruition of the beauty he had
hoped they might reveal to others, but which they
had in fact often obscured so sadly even from himself.

Yet the central word about Blake can never be a
word of depreciation. It can never cease to be true
of him that he embodied and proclaimed at its purest
the impulse of which all art is the issue, and raising
art, as all the greatest artists do, to a level with the
noblest achievements of the human spirit, showed that
in its essence the artistic principle is the very principle
of life itself; and that all religion, all conduct, are
barren and profitless except in so far as they express
it. He is, of course, greatest both as a man and an
artist when circumstances allow him to exemplify
rather than to uphold this truth; and it was his life's
misfortune that circumstances enabled him to exemplify it so seldom and forced him to waste so much
of his energy in upholding it. He was driven, in the

bulk of his work, to a passionate vindication of the inmost principle of his being; he did not see that it ceased to show the qualities he claimed for it in proportion to the necessity he found of claiming them. But the work which puts Blake among the immortals is his *Songs of Innocence.* Innocence is his secret; as life becomes a problem to him, the problem presents itself simply as the search for a means to preserve innocence in all the freshness and purity of its youth—

> Youth of delight, come hither,
> And see the opening morn,
> Image of truth new-born.

And he is great, he is among the greatest, because although the secret is often obscured and buried in his art, he yet knew how to keep himself, as a man, in living touch with it, so that to the end of his life, in spite of the prejudices and arrogance of his egotism, and in the very hour of death itself, he was a child.

It is in the *Songs of Innocence,* then, and whatever other song, or fragment of song, whatever painting, drawing, or decorative design he may have conceived in the same spirit, it is in these that Blake's immortality is to be looked for, in these that he possesses, with the complete, the indefinable possession of the artist, that spring of life which most of his

QUEEN KATHARINE'S VISION

GEORGE A. MACMILLAN, ESQ.

To face p. 29

after years were spent in unavailing efforts to recover. The purity and rapture of his early vision were so little appreciated or understood that there can be small matter for wonder if Blake was ready to stray from the green pastures of delight into the wildernesses of conflict and justification. And the principle he undertook to justify was, if we may so phrase it, unjustifiable : its justification had lain in its existence, and to explain was to destroy it. For the spirit of Blake's songs, and of his exquisite flower-like designs, perfect as it is, is an unconscious perfection, the perfection rather of the seed than of the tree ; and to plant the seed is to place it in conditions which call upon it imperiously to pass out of itself. The powers of life and development have been set in motion ; the effort to evade them can only result in a wayward stunted growth. Blake's theory of art and conduct is the expression of the life-principle from which art and conduct grow and without which they cannot be ; pure, with the purity of his own childlike spirit ; but in its very purity formless, undeveloped, unanalysable, and just in so far as he insists on analysing it, profitless and false. Thus while the wide and searching appeal, of which Blake's message is more and more showing itself a vehicle, depends on the discovery by him of something essential, implicit in the human mind; on the worship of that life-force, that longing for the light, which all our growth and expansion presuppose; the same appeal is the more apt to waste itself the more deeply it drives home and the stimulus it gives to issue in a mere maze of blind impulse and confusion, because it completely fails to take cognisance of the ascertained conditions under which growth goes on. The expanding principle, life, innocence, takes form as it expands; and its form is determined by its experience; but experience is not innocence inverted, as Blake supposed it to be. Experience is not a denial, and to curse it is to curse innocence itself.

But it is time to leave paradox and turn to a more sympathetic appreciation of the truth which Blake embodied in his art, and attempted, with all the passion and energy of his soul, to formulate in his philosophy. To Blake, the secret of life was joy, an unfettered expansion of the soul, the human spirit passing out into the world, entering into all it found there, embracing all, loving all, and needing no restriction except what came to it from the inner principle of its own life, from the love of which all life was the expression.

> Arise you little glancing wings and sing your infant joy!
> Arise and drink your bliss, for everything that lives is holy!

"LORD, TEACH THESE SOULS TO FLY"
BRITISH MUSEUM

To face p. 30

Life was not life to him, unless, as from a deep internal
source, this joy of love welled up in it with a perpetual
overflow.   In his early years he knew, as few can have
known it, that trance-like exquisite delight which is
the soul's assurance that the earth is its true home,
that its loves cannot pass unrequited, that its whole
desire will find satisfaction at last; and even the
beauty of the earth was itself seen by him as the veil
to a greater beauty, as God in His mercy drew the
soul to the more perfect revelation of Himself.   The
negro mother explains it to her little boy :

> Look on the rising sun,—there God does live,
>   And gives his light, and gives his heat away ;
> And flowers and trees and beasts and men receive
>   Comfort in morning, joy in the noonday.
>
> And we are put on earth a little space,
>   That we may learn to bear the beams of love ;
> And these black bodies and this sun-burnt face
>   Is but a cloud, and like a shady grove.
>
> For when our souls have learn'd the heat to bear,
>   The cloud will vanish, we shall hear His voice,
> Saying : " Come out from the grove, My love and care,
>   And round My golden tent like lambs rejoice."

This was the fountain of Blake's inspiration, and
his life's battle was fought to preserve its strength and

purity untouched. He saw the human soul enveloped
and sustained by a beauty too great to be borne, and
he never lost faith in the reality of that sustaining
presence. It was the only reality to him. A true life,
he believed, would be pervaded by the sense of it; it
would be a life of ecstasy, passed in direct continuous
communion with God. " Do you work with fear and
trembling?" Blake asked in late life of his young
disciple Palmer. " Yes, indeed," said Palmer. " Then
you'll do," was Blake's reply; and "just before he died,
his countenance became fair, his eyes brightened, and
he burst out into singing of the things he saw in
heaven." Blake's immortality is the blossoming of this
joy. When he was not fighting against impulses that
seemed to threaten it, or denouncing an age by which
it could not be understood, when this joy and this alone
possessed him, words flowed from his lips, form and
colour grew under his hand, which for all time breathe
forth a radiance of communion, the very life-breath of
that artist for whom action, thought, and love, were one.

> ' I have no name :
>   I am but two days old.'
>   What shall I call thee ?
> ' I happy am,
>   Joy is my name.'
>   Sweet joy befall thee !

This joy was Blake's inspiration, and as life opened
wider aspects before him, and he grew conscious of his
inspiration and was able to reflect upon it, the same joy
became his gospel. He preached the gospel of Innocence.

But, of course, the *Songs of Innocence* must not be
thought of as in themselves exhausting the fountain of
Blake's artistic impulse. Its strength may be taken as
typified in them, because they express it in the sweetest,
the fairest, the freshest of all the forms he ever gave to
it. But the spirit of innocence, as understood by Blake,
was not restricted for companionship to children, angels,
and lambs ; neither must we look only to the *Songs* for
its expression. Rather is it to be conceived as that
spirit for which the wolf dwells with the lamb, and the
leopard lies down with the kid, and the calf and the
young lion and the fatling together, because there is a
little child to lead them. " Those things which are
called Vices in the Natural World are the highest
sublimities in the Spiritual World," Blake assured his
hesitating admirer, Crabb Robinson, and we may
imagine the assurance given with an inviting smile, as
if it were a Daniel doing the honours in his den. Much
of the theory so forcibly enunciated in the *Marriage of
Heaven and Hell* is an elaboration of the same idea,
expressed there with the recklessness and flourish

c

appropriate to an inferior type of lion-tamer. Innocence, at this stage, is almost ostentatiously at home in
Hell, where " it walks among the flames, and delights
in the enjoyments of genius." "The reason Milton
wrote in fetters when he wrote of Angels and God, and
at liberty when of Devils and Hell, is that he was a
true poet, and of the Devil's party without knowing
it." "Enough or too much" is the Devil's leading
motto, and his only principle of morality that of the
confectioner, who, to prevent filching, grants his assis-
tants an unlimited supply of sweets. "Dip him in the
river who loves water." "If the fool would persist in
his folly, he would become wise." "Exuberance is
Beauty." The last quotation brings us directly into
touch with the principle of innocence as Blake more
widely applied it. His one test is spontaneity, the
unrestricted flow of living natural desire ; an excess in
this true overflow was impossible to him to conceive :
and as usual, if we take his words in the narrow context
to which they are really applicable, we find that he is
right. This innocent unbounded selflessness is the
only sure principle of artistic workmanship ; and in
applying it to Blake's own work, we are at once able to
distinguish false from true. It is of course in his
bolder, more tumultuous creations that his directness
of inspiration generally falters. Two exquisite lines in

"OBERON AND TITANIA"
BRITISH MUSEUM

To face p. 35

his poem of *The Four Zoas* can hardly fail to have been
suggested to him by the two principal aspects of his
own work :

At will to murmur in the flowers, small as the honey
bee,
At will to stretch across the heavens, and step from
star to star.

Blake has drawings—it is needless to name them—
which justify the second of these lines, but compared
with the number of his efforts in that direction, they
are surprisingly few. His powers of spiritual conquest,
in the annihilation of space and time, had a fascinating
influence upon him, which led him to overreach himself in his employment of them. They lost spontaneity
partly because they became a subject of too constant
reflection, partly—to be quite candid—because he was
conceited about them and adopted a forcing artificial
method. An attack was thus made from two sides
upon the fountains of his innocence. The result was a
series of nightmare visions, in which violence is substituted for exuberance, and the spirit of liberty attempts
to override restrictions by hypocritically denying that
they exist. " He who can be bound down is no genius.
Genius cannot be bound. Opposition makes the wise
man mad." It is indeed in his theory and demonstra-

tion of his own genius that Blake walks over the line, and perhaps it is only when he is at his gentlest that he is ever perfectly secure. For the rest, an occasional burst of rocket brilliance, or thunder of inspired artillery, but as a rule more smoke than brightness and a pervasive taint of explosives upon the air.

Yet it must never be forgotten—those who know Blake intimately can indeed never forget—that it was, after all, by the depth and security of his hold on truth, where he had it, by the convincing reality of his inspiration, when it came, that he was enabled to stray so far from the one, to confuse so much that was perfervid and paltry with the other, without being aware what he was doing. This too was a part of his innocence, and came of that child-like vein in him to which the loveliest and most lasting qualities in his work are due. His art and his religion went hand in hand all through his life; and though he was not without the self-assertiveness common to individuals who claim a divine revelation, he yet knew where to turn when the strength and buoyancy of his heart and mind grew dim. Gilchrist relates how Richmond, " finding his invention flag during a whole fortnight, went to Blake, as was his wont, for some advice or comfort. He found him sitting at tea with his wife. He related his distress; how he felt deserted

by the power of invention.   To his astonishment,
Blake turned to his wife suddenly and said : 'It is just
so with us, is it not, for weeks together, when the
visions forsake us ?   What do we do then, Kate ?'
' We kneel down and pray, Mr. Blake.'"   Not from the
mere words, but from the homeliness of their setting,
the sympathy which prompted them, the spirit of rest
and confidence which they express, a new vision, and
yet what is without doubt the nearest to a true vision
of Blake, the "real Blake," rises before our eyes.   As
in the bulk of his work he is made known to us, Blake
has not a little of the fierce formlessness of the Minotaur
about him, and, if we strive to track him to his lair, for
the most part we do but risk our lives in the inextric-
able windings of his labyrinth.   But here it seems we
have stumbled upon the well of living water, which the
labyrinth itself was reared to honour, which all the
Minotaur's ferocity was summoned to protect.   And
having reached it, we shall not need to wander more.

CHAPTER III

BLAKE'S CONCEPTION OF LOVE

BLAKE'S theories are only seen in their true light when
related to the mental atmosphere which produced them.
Truth is complex and many-sided; and when a man
whose intellectual power is above the average is able to
throw the whole of his weight on one side of a question,
we shall find, almost invariably, that he is pitting himself, consciously or unconsciously, against a society
whose weight is thrown upon the other; and this will
hold good in a peculiar degree of that part of his
theory which he is content to assert and does not proceed to act on. Blake was an impassioned advocate of
free love; he consistently upheld the essential purity
of the sexual instinct; he spoke of abstinence with
scorn, and associated chastity with ideas for which
he had nothing but contempt. Our society of to-day
is more familiar with these ideas than the society to
which Blake first addressed them. M. Maeterlinck can
avail himself of the weight and traditional influence

of the *Fortnightly Review* when he wishes to congratulate himself and his contemporaries upon the disappearance of chastity from modern life. " Nous ne sommes plus chastes," he writes, with a sublime complacency; and his readers, few of whom, under present conditions, can quite ignore what promiscuity is, or where it leads to, naturally blink a little when they find that Blake, to whom they look back as the herald of this gospel, lived a long life in unbroken conjugal fidelity, and was a perfect model of domestic dulness.

The key to Blake's position may be found in a delicate little lyric headed *To My Myrtle*, and so short that it can be quoted here entire:

> To a lovely myrtle bound,
> Blossoms show'ring all around,
> Oh how sick and weary I
> Underneath my myrtle lie!
> Why should I be bound to thee,
> O my lovely myrtle-tree?

This reads, at first sight, merely as an attack on marriage, to be dismissed as petulant by those who reverence marriage, and hailed with acclaim by all who chafe under what they consider unreasonable restrictions. The latter read little but the third line of the piece,

taking the rest vaguely as an atmosphere, except for a
climax at the beginning of line five, where an impressive
emphasis is placed upon the word " why." But to take it
thus is to mistake it. Blake is not searching here for
the reason of the marriage-tie ; a general prejudice
against reason kept him from such a search. His purpose is subtler. He reiterates two ideas : that his
myrtle-tree is beautiful, but that he is bound to it. It
is because he is bound that he is sick and weary,
and he chafes, not because he wishes to go elsewhere,
but because he wishes to stay where he is ; and, being
conscious of that wish, resents a bond that robs his
allegiance of its spontaneity and grace. This is so
simple and childlike as to verge on childishness. But
it is Blake. " Do you think," he once said, " if I came
home and discovered my wife to be unfaithful, I should
be so foolish as to take it ill ? " The logic of Blake's
dream-world often savours more than a little of that of
a more familiar Wonderland. We must remember that
it was a part of his principles never to be put out. He
has much of the meandering mildness of the mock-
turtle. Who else could have provided this question
with an appropriate repartee ?

The quality of Blake's allegiance came at one time to
the test, and in his poem, *William Bond*, Blake records
and attempts to universalise the experience he then

passed through.[1] The poem defies consistent inter-pretation, because one part of it is, undoubtedly, drawn from a recollection of particular events not known and not revealed to the reader, and another part from the vaguer symbolical world, with which for Blake these events were associated, and where they run parallel with much to which the uninitiate would never dream of coupling them. But the principal truth stands out clearly ; that the grace and spontaneity of Blake's allegiance faltered : these happy " fairies " left him, and he found their place taken by the "angels of Providence," emissaries of him to whom Convention kneels. He admits the change to his wife with a beautiful sincerity. And the revelation of loyalty in her which comes to him at the sight of her distress, and the fact of that distress itself, change him and restore the perfect spontaneity of his love.

> Mary trembled and Mary chill'd,
> And Mary fell down on the right-hand floor,
> That William Bond and his sister Jane
> Scarce could recover Mary more.

[1] The reasons adduced by Messrs. Ellis and Yeats to show that this poem is not to be read in connection with Blake's married life appear trivial to the present writer. The mystical scheme, which they have worked out, must remain of greatest service to students of Blake's work ; but it is a cumbrous weapon, and it often seems as if the whole strength of its discoverers were exhausted in the mere attempt to brandish it.

When Mary woke and found her laid
On the right hand of her William dear,
On the right-hand of his lovèd bed,
And saw her William Bond so near,

The fairies that fled from William Bond
Dancèd around her shining head,
They dancèd over the pillow white,
And the angels of Providence left the bed.

Thus a new quality is revealed to him in the nature of
love itself : and this, leaving now the particular experience, he universalises in words that have the beauty
and tenderness of a caress :

I thought Love lived in the hot sunshine,
But oh, he lives in the moony light !
I thought to find Love in the heat of day,
But sweet Love is the comforter of night.

Seek Love in the pity of others' woe,
In the gentle relief of another's care,
In the darkness of night and the winter's snow,
In the naked and outcast, seek Love there !

Blake's general outlook upon life was of a kind likely
to render a clear statement of his ideas upon the sexual
problem singularly difficult to him.   He was, intellectually, what the philosophers call a subjective idealist.
He believed that for each several man nothing existed

except the content of his own mind : his own body, with the world it moved in, and all that he might naturally tend to speak of as other than, outside, himself, was illusory, unreal ; the mind alone was real, and each man's mind was his universe. Speaking then as a philosopher, Blake had the right to say that what we call the body does not exist. It exists, he would say, only as an idea in the mind ; and, of course, when we speak of the body, that is not what we ordinarily mean to convey. Speaking as a poet, however—or, rather, feeling and living as a poet—he was conscious, as all poets are, of the immense significance of the purely physical activities, of the thrill of pleasure and refreshment which accompanies all bodily exercises as such. And this consciousness led him — in his less philosophic moments—to speak of the body as the only source of life, and, without troubling to look for any distinction between one and another kind of physical activity, to praise all unrestrictedly and with an undiscriminating enthusiasm. " Energy is eternal delight." His philosophic doctrine, that the body had no real existence, helped to conceal the mental confusion in which such a position really involved him. The body being, after all, a mere nonentity, it mattered very little what you thought or said about it.

A further element of confusion was introduced into

Blake's mind by influences reflected from the mystical scheme in which he habitually clothed his abstract thought.   Love was to him the crown of all things, the one right attitude of heart and mind, the only true humanity.   It stood to the whole life of man in the same relation as that occupied in the artist's life by the creative imaginative power.   And the artist's life being to Blake an epitome of the whole life of man at its best and highest, the power of love and the power of imaginative creation came to be regarded by him as identical. Both had the faculty, which nothing else on earth seemed to possess, of bringing the soul into direct touch with God, rousing man to a realisation of the divine power that was at work within him.   Wherever Blake theorises about life, he makes it clear that nothing has value for him but the conscious exercise of one or other of these powers.   He does not stop to consider whether the unillumined moments, and the attitude of mind in which they are regarded, may have their bearing upon the quality or content of the illumination when it comes.   The life is the illumination.   The intervals are negligible: man vegetates in them, he does not live; and in so far as any legacy from the unillumined state, any residue of routine thinking, obtrudes itself upon the spirit in its hour of freedom, there is no occasion, in Blake's view, for reasonable inquiry into the cause of such a mishap; the only possible course of action is to utter imprecations against mankind for possessing any other than the poetic or artistic faculties. Thus Blake's morality, like his artistic theory, is based on the presupposition that a continuous exercise of the highest powers is the only conceivable ideal of human life, and that in our attitude to conduct day by day we ought to recognise this ideal as realisable, and regulate our effort accordingly. The true artist is always imaginative, the true man is a constant overflow of love. Now, mystically, just as love was, to Blake, imagination as it appears in conduct, so was imagination the mental counterpart of love. And the term love, in this connection, included for him its sexual expression:

> Wherever beauty appears,
> If in the morning sun I find it, there my eyes are fix'd
> In happy copulation: if in evening mild, wearied with work
> Sit on a bank and draw the pleasures of this free-born joy.

Nor is this parallel confined to a poetic imagery. It is worked into an elaborate symbolic scheme. The imaginative mind is male. Space, or the world of Nature, is female. The history of poetic-inspiration is the history of their loves. And the consummation which the artist looks for is the entire subjection of the feminine principle, its reduction to perfect malleability before the ardours of imagination. " There is no such thing in eternity as a female will."

But it must be clear that in exact proportion to the degree in which imagery of this kind is allowed to stereotype itself, it loses its illuminative power and degenerates into foolishness; and the sexual analogies pervade Blake's mysticism. Aiming at a kind of imaginative transcendentalism, he fell so low as to destroy imaginative truth by literalising it and reducing it to a rule of thumb. Like all idealists, he saw mind as the measure of all things. He believes himself to be reiterating this truth when he asserts that to the ultimate imaginative understanding there is only one form in Nature— that everything appears to it as a Man. The nature of man admits of a threefold division into head, heart, and loins; the same division is recognisable every- where; everywhere the problem of life is to place these three parts in their true relations one to another, to resolve their antagonisms, to lift them into unity. Thus the one problem of life becomes a problem of sex. The problem is attacked by Blake from the most exalted standpoint possible, and solved by him in a purely spiritual sense; and partly because of this exaltation of mind, which was a second nature to him, he gives his solution in a form which makes it safe to be misinterpreted by those who take his words in their more normal setting.   Moreover—and this is more immediately to our point—Blake's mystical introduction of sexual analogies in departments of life to which they were not proper, naturally led him, in consideration of the sexual nature itself, to bring back from those other departments, and treat as sexual, qualities that belonged in reality to them alone.   How is an analogy to be universalised and worked out in every part, unless by successive acts of mental violence, which only set up a likeness by obscuring points of difference? When Blake spoke of the sexual nature, what was before him was a confused creature of his own mind, crusted over, like Proteus, with every kind of alien growth, with the shells and seaweed of spurious metaphor which by degrees had attached themselves to him as he groped his way submerged in the ocean depths of a self-made mythology.

All this must be remembered before Blake's pronouncements on the relations of the sexes can become explicable or be seen in any relation to the rest of life. And we must remember also that the problem, in its practical bearings, was one which Blake's whole mental habit made it impossible for him to approach. The problem is essentially a social problem, and Blake, both in theory and in temperament, was a pure individualist. Only once in the whole course of his writing do we find him recognising any value in law or social compact, and that is in a poem the subject of which is the game of blind man's buff!

> " Such," he writes, " are the fortunes of the game
> And those who play should stop the same
> By wholesome laws : such as, all those
> Who on the blinded man impose
> Stand in his stead."

When he came to view the more serious organisation of society, he failed to understand that it must involve similar requirements, and of a more complicated kind. Rather one may say that the organisation of society was a thing which never came within his view at all. He saw one truth only—that to restrict an impulse is to change its nature. He refused to believe in the existence of an unholy impulse. Man's whole desire is for the good. It is only by being thwarted and fettered that he becomes base. Sin is the child of the law.

> I wander thro' each charter'd street,
> Near where the charter'd Thames does flow,
> And mark in every face I meet
> Marks of weakness, marks of woe.

In every cry of every man,
In every infant's cry of fear,
In every voice, in every ban,
The mind-forg'd manacles I hear.

How the chimney-sweeper's cry
Every black'ning church appals ;
And the hapless soldier's sigh
Runs in blood down palace walls.

But most thro' midnight streets I hear
How the youthful harlot's curse
Blasts the new-born infant's tear,
And blights with plagues the marriage hearse.

This belief was not, of course, of Blake's own forming.
It was of the spirit of the French Revolution. It was
part of the very air he breathed. He believed, as so
many have believed, as so many are once more trying
to believe now, that the gift of freedom is in itself
the gift of truth. He believed that love and desire,
horrible in their division, are divided only because an
external artificial check is placed upon them when they
appear, as they appear first, in their natural unity.

I cry Love ! Love ! Love ! happy, happy Love .
free as the mountain wind !

To rob love of its expression was to change desire into
a venomous, rankling introspection, which contaminated

D

all it touched; and harlotry came of the attempt to bind man's nature down with the chains of an impossible abstinence, from which, when it broke away, it broke away only into sin.

The truth contained in all this is truth of a limited kind, and, so far as Blake applies it to the normal constitution of society, it is misapplied. He is giving, in confused contexts, the experience of his own highly sensitive, impulsive, idealistic nature. In average humanity the sexual impulse is something much closer to the desire for an animal satisfaction, and the checks which social life imposes on such satisfaction, and the need to control the desire which follows from them, are in effect one of the chief influences by which the animal impulse becomes spiritualised and recognisable as worthy of the name of love. But Blake's utterances were not the outcome of any kind of unprejudiced observation of average human nature; like all anarchists, he proceeded on the assumption that his own experience and his own ideal were the only ideals and experience conceivable. His ideas on the subject of sex have therefore no bearing upon the broader social question; they have little significance, except in their relation to the aspirations and difficulties that belong to the religious and artistic temperament. Taking them in this relation, and separating them from the mass of mystical and symbolical associations with which we generally find them accompanied, we can recognise the core of Blake's belief to be, here as everywhere, a horror of any kind of external restraint, or artificial tampering with the natural impulses of the soul : the artist lives not by self-denial, but by self-surrender. And he was able to formulate his doctrine without reserve, to carry it, regardless of any possible mitigations of circumstance, to the most astounding conclusions, to vaunt himself before the eyes of the world in language often undistinguishable from what might be used by the most careless of libertines, because, in the first place, his traditions of life and personal habits were overwhelmingly on the side of order, and, still more, in the second place, because the whole trend of his nature was deeply spiritual and spiritually unified, so that the problem of desire was never viewed by him from below, but always from above. Thus the region of thought in which he was moving was a region which could never be reached except by a man for whom checks, which operate on a lower level to restrain the coarser kinds of lawlessness, had ceased to have a meaning ; and if, when he theorises, he permits himself to denounce those checks, we do not take his deeper meaning until we see that he is doing himself an injustice, and, out of pure simple-mindedness, leaving the better half of his nature unexpressed; only, indeed, because it is too much a part of himself to need conscious expression.

> Can I see another's woe,
> And not be in sorrow too?
> Can I see another's grief,
> And not seek for kind relief?
>
> Can I see a falling tear,
> And not feel my sorrow's share?
> No, no! never can it be!
> Never, never can it be!

The poem of *William Bond* seems to show that sentiments of this kind were something better than sentiments, as Blake made use of them; they divide him sharply from the more modern advocates of the theory of free love. Blake was thus fortified on the one side by the fact that it was impossible to him to be consciously the cause of unhappiness in another. Love needed no bonds in him, and he called for freedom for it because, as he knew it, it was complete, and spontaneously, as it expressed itself, observed the higher laws of its nature. On the other side, he was fortified by the transcendent claims of his idealism. Passion was to him the very spirit of life; he would nowhere have it bound down; and we only understand his refusal to restrict it in remembering that he knew himself intimately in touch with ends as high as any that it can be made to serve, and that it was on these that his energy and desire were concentrated. " Men are admitted into heaven, not because they have curbed and governed their passions, but because they have cultivated their understandings. The treasures of heaven are not negations of passion, but realities of intellect, from which all the passions emanate, uncurbed in their eternal glory." " We are told to abstain from fleshly desires that we may lose no time from the work of the Lord. Every moment lost is a moment that cannot be redeemed ; every pleasure that intermingles with the duty of our station is a folly unredeemable, and is planted like the seed of a wild flower among our wheat. . . . I know of no other Christianity and of no other gospel than the liberty both of body and mind to exercise the Divine Arts of Imagination. What is the Life of Man but Art and Science ? Is it Meat and Drink ? What is mortality, but the things relating to the body which dies ? What is Immortality, but the things relating to the Spirit, which lives eternally ? " But the root of Blake's position will only become finally clear to those who, having first a sufficient acquaintance with the outlines of his system and his individual methods of expression, turn to the copy of Swedenborg's *Angelic Wisdom concerning the Divine Love*, with Blake's marginal notes, preserved now in the British Museum. Swedenborg puts the life of man upon three planes, or in three degrees: the natural, the rational, the spiritual; and in the early part of his treatise Blake takes him to be suggesting that a man can pass out of the lower into the higher by, as it were, exhausting the lower and therefore leaving it behind him. Blake will have none of this: "Study science till you are blind; study intellectuals till you are cold; yet science cannot teach intellect, much less can intellect teach affection." His comments are highly critical, discriminative, and disparaging. But as the book goes on he comes to see that Swedenborg's position is really the same as his own; and though he has, in consequence, less to say upon the margins, his writing smiles and expands, and he makes it very clear that his deepest convictions are now being expressed. *Swedenborg:* "The understanding does not bend the will. Wisdom does not produce love." *Blake:* "Mark this." *Swedenborg:* "The love or will is defiled in the understanding and by it, if they are not elevated together." *Blake:* "Mark this. They are elevated together." Love is, for Blake, the principle of life, the beginning and the end of life, at once immanent and transcending. Man is not man, except as

THE SOUL AND THE DIVINE LOVE
CAPTAIN ARCHIBALD STIRLING

To face p. 55

he yields his spirit to its influence; he cannot rise to any spiritual joy or wisdom, unless he is guided and inspired by love. There is a kind of life, calling itself moral, that seems as if it could be lived without it; there is an abstract reason that robs life of its warmth and dictates to men the course of action they would be right to follow if their hearts were not warm, but cold. But the human heart is not cold, it is warm; and it is better—Blake's last word is here—to be sinful, so only that we keep it warm, than to freeze it with the banns of a Pharisaical holiness, shutting out the divine radiance and heat. There is beauty in the very fact of sin itself, when it opens the heart to a new vision of the depth and tenderness of love. " O Mercy, O Divine Humanity, O Forgiveness, and Pity, and Compassion, if I were Pure I should never have known thee, if I were unpolluted I should never have glorified thy holiness or rejoiced in thy great Salvation."

CHAPTER IV

BLAKE'S MADNESS

WAS Blake mad? The question is unpopular, yet all
the vociferation of Blake's admirers has not been able
to silence it. Those who defend Blake's sanity with
the greatest fervour are often more compromising in
their statements than his direct opponents; and it is
certain that nothing defeats its own end more completely than an apologia which takes refuge in violent
assertion that no apology is needed. Blake's work,
both in art and literature, is of a kind that obliges
him to come before the public apologetically, and to
deny this is to do him no real service. It is not only
bad criticism, it is bad pleading. Obviously, till we
know what to think of Blake in this particular, appreciation of his achievement loses half its value. But
what is madness? It is a kind of unreasonableness, no
doubt; yet everybody is unreasonable at times, and
when we come to look for it we find that no clear
boundary line between sane and insane is to be found.

The area of neutral territory is immense. Most of us are sane occasionally, and we are all sometimes mad. The early idea of Blake was that he was "odd," "a little touched in his head." This, of course, will not do. Blake was a great man, possessed of high susceptibility to beauty and rare moral and intellectual power. He needs to be dealt with on rather larger lines.

The most commonly accepted sign of madness is incoherence. Truth is a system; and if the individual mind reflects this system justly, its thoughts will fit together, or, at least, since the parts of the system reflected in them may not be adjacent, can be made to fit when missing links have been supplied. Blake's early critics supposed that in the world of the mind he was an aimless wanderer. His perversity, in the abuse of language, and the paradoxical nature of his thought, made such a supposition pardonable. But it has been the principal achievement of more recent criticism to show that Blake's utterances, whatever else they may have been, were not disjointed. Messrs. Ellis and Yeats quote *Hamlet* on the title-page of their monumental work; and Professor Raleigh, after repeating the quotation, proclaims Blake to be "one of the boldest, most spontaneous, and most consistent of English poets and thinkers. There is no part of his writings, no casual recorded saying or scribbled note on the margins of the books he read, which is not of a piece with all the rest. An absolute unity of character and purpose runs through all." This is true; criticism has finally established it; yet in a poet—Professor Raleigh would be the first to admit the point—there is something forbidding, something fell, in a consistency so perfect. And after all, is not Blake, half the time, rigid rather than spontaneous in his consistency? In much that he says he is at one with all leaders of spiritual insight, and if we understand them we understand him also. In the rest it is the consistency that is the trouble. In a great artist, it is often his very inconsistency which we bow before, because we know it to be the sign of a more commanding vision. Who bothers his head to inquire if Shakespeare was consistent? If we want to know whether a man is to be relied on as a thinker, coherence is the test; but if we want to know whether an artist has seen the divine truth and beauty, the test is different. Indeed, nothing is more damaging to the value of Blake's visionary experiences than this fact which modern criticism has discovered so triumphantly about them, that they are all of a piece. Moreover, it should be remembered that the madness of coherence is a quite familiar type. There is the case of the lady who consistently believed herself to be the king's sister, the

RICHARD III. AND THE GHOSTS OF HIS VICTIMS

George A. Macmillan, Esq.

illusion being serious only because it was not transitory and expressed itself in everything that she did. If there was any madness in Blake at all it was clearly of the latter kind. There is discomfort in the handling of this theme because the process involves us in a certain seriousness of attitude not quite appropriate to it. Blake's claims were extravagant; and the gentlest and surely the truest way of meeting them would be to set them aside as a part merely of his childishness; as the great defect of his great merit; to treat them in fact as irrelevancies and say no more about them. Yet the bulk of his work undoubtedly takes its colour from these claims and from his conviction that they were well founded. And this conviction communicates itself to many of his admirers. It must be admitted then that the point about which the problem centres is Blake's attitude to what he called his revelation and the effect of this attitude upon his visions.

There is a tendency in modern thought to set the idea of revelation on one side, because it seems to involve a machinery for conveying truth which is incompatible with the nature of truth itself. But, granted it be possible, revelation as revelation is only for the man to whom it is immediately made. It cannot be transmitted to others except through the mind of the recipient, and in the process of transmission its

character is necessarily changed. Others are obliged
to judge of it according to a standard of intrinsic
reasonableness, without considering its claim to a
peculiar sanction. Moreover, the fact that a visionary
believes in himself is not to be regarded as particularly
significant. There has been so-called revelation of
pure nonsense. The main point is that the same
critical method that would be employed to estimate
the value of any other expression of religious or artistic
truth must be applied to the content of revelation also.
We do not need to engage in metaphysical contro-
versies, or to define our attitude to visions in general ;
we only need to ask whether or not there were the
evidences of reasonableness in Blake's attitude to his.

Every one, of course, now knows that the language
in which Blake thought right to dwell on his poetic
visions was the language of religious ecstasy. In a
famous letter addressed to Hayley in the year 1805 he
writes, " It will not be long before I shall be able to
present the full history of my spiritual sufferings to the
dwellers upon earth, and of the spiritual victories
obtained for me by my friends. Excuse this effusion
of the spirit from one who cares little for this world
which passes away, whose happiness is secured in Jesus
our Lord, and who looks for suffering till the time of
complete deliverance." Or again, in a letter to Butts

(April 1803), " None can know the spiritual acts of my
three years' slumber on the banks of ocean unless he
has seen them in the spirit, or unless he should read my
long poem descriptive of those acts; for I have in these
years composed an immense number of verses on one
grand theme, similar to Homer's *Iliad* or Milton's
Paradise Lost. . . . I mention this to show you what I
think the grand reason of my being brought down here.
I have a thousand and ten thousand things to say to
you. My heart is full of futurity. I perceive that the
sore travail which has been given me these three years
leads to glory and honour. I rejoice and tremble; ' I
am fearfully and wonderfully made.' I had been reading the 139th Psalm a little before your letter arrived.
I take your advice. I see the face of my Heavenly
Father. He lays His hand upon my head, and gives a
blessing to all my work." These passages represent
Blake's normal attitude to his prophetic writing; and
nothing in them comes out more triumphantly than
the complete serenity of his self-confidence. There
was no shadow of doubt in him that he was inspired,
and that his visions were as authentic as those of the
prophets of old. " Mark my words," he reiterates in
the *Milton*, " they are for your eternal salvation." It
cannot, I think, be necessary to mention Blake's name
by the side of the names of Isaiah and Ezekiel to see

that there is here a false note struck. Blake's visions can never come to be recognised as based upon the same order of spiritual insight as theirs ; but if they cannot, while yet to Blake himself it is a matter of triumphant conviction that they can, and if this false conviction is a ruling conviction of his life, I do not see that his admirers have any serious right to complain if the charge of madness is brought against him.

Approaching the subject more in detail we note in the first place that Blake repeatedly shows a complete lack of discrimination in his use of the language of fervour, and will speak with the same intensity of objects that might be supposed worthy of it and others which manifestly are not so. The reader of the Prophetic Books often suspects that a confusion of this kind is taking place, and Blake's reputation is only saved there by his unintelligibility : the error cannot easily be brought home to him. It is, however, clearly exemplified in the letter to Hayley from which I have already quoted. Not content to speak of his own visions as inspired, he lifts the work of Hayley—which he ordinarily regarded with scathing contempt—on to the same plane : " It is the greatest of crimes to depress true art and science. I know that those who are dead from the earth and who mocked and despised the meek. ness of true art (and such, I find, has been the situation

of our beautiful affectionate ballads), I know that such
mockers are most severely punished in eternity. I
know it, for I see it, and dare not help. The mocker
of art is the mocker of Jesus. Let us go on, dear Sir,
following his Cross . . . ." No one knew better than
Blake that Hayley's work had nothing to do either
with true science or true art. "How wide the gulf
and impassable between simplicity and insipidity," he
writes at the opening of the second book of his *Milton*
in a reference that no one can mistake. And thus the
language of his letter, though affecting and beautiful
in its ingenuousness, puts it beyond doubt that in these
times of transport Blake is not to be relied on for any
power of relating his ideas to appropriate objects, or
finding worthy embodiment for his emotion. In the
letter quoted we find him on the borders of his dream-
world and it is a fact not to be glossed over that he can
use the most sacred of its symbols with utter recklessness. Had his ecstasy been resting upon a sane and
sure foundation, had the spirit he speaks of been before
his mind and entering into his words, would this recklessness have been possible to him? The question
surely admits only of one reply.

Turning to the Prophetic Books themselves, we find
the integrity of inspiration which Blake claims for them
threatened everywhere by a similar incontinence of

emotional expression. Questioned as to the source of his spiritual second-sight, Blake answered : " You have only to work up imagination to the state of vision, and the thing is done." He accurately described his own achievement, but the description has its unhappy aspect. We get a picture of the lion lashing his sides with his tail, provoking himself to an artificial fervour. And to the reader of Blake's prophetic books this image will frequently recur. Their atmosphere is an artificial atmosphere ; its heat for the most part mechanically superinduced upon lifeless material. The least significant of actions, the mildest of purposes, not only tasks a giant to fulfil it, but is usually approached by the destined operator in a state of impetuous if not ungovernable fury ; or if the passion is genuinely mild it will have the mildness of languorous abandonment, and will equally be described at its extreme. These meltings, groanings, burnings, howlings, and all this violence of hate, jealousy, and love are a mere fantasy. As for artistic effect, such extravagance destroys all possibility of it. With every allowance for the unintelligibility of the language, its unrelieved intensity is a sufficient test ; the normal mind cannot assimilate more than two pages of Blake's prophecy without sensations approaching nausea. Clearly these facts afford no evidence for supposing that the writer's feelings were maintained at so high a pitch by superhuman agency. The reverse is the truth.

Again, there is little doubt that Blake's belief in himself as called to prophesy led him to take the Hebrew writers as models of prophetic expression; and many of the eccentricities of his nomenclature are due to the fact that it is derivative and unintelligently derived. If we turn the pages of Isaiah we come on sentences such as this: " And Heshbon shall cry and Elealah; their voice shall be heard even unto Jahaz; thereupon the armed soldiers of Moab shall cry out; his life shall be grievous unto him." Following the Swedenborgian system of Biblical interpretation Blake was led to believe that there was a mystic significance in these names, as names used for their own sake ; and with this principle in view, he writes : " Till Canaan rolled apart from Albion across the Rhine along the Danube, and all the land of Canaan suspended over the Valley of Cheviot from Bashan to Tyre and from Troy to Gaza of the Amalekites." It must be borne in mind that the writings of the prophets were far more unintelligible in Blake's day than they are now, and there seems little doubt that Blake accepted this unintelligibility as part of the evidence of their supernatural origin : " allegory addressed to the intellectual powers while it is altogether hid from the corporeal under-

E

standing is my definition of the sublimest poetry " he writes in a letter to Butts ; and it is clear from this that he had come to regard unintelligibility as essential to the poetical and the sublime.   That the Hebrew prophets are obscure to us in our time because they wrote at another time for other men and spoke of details which were then familiar but are lost now in complete oblivion, this seems not to have occurred to Blake.   Of course the original value of the prophecy lay in its living grasp of the contemporary issue ; it is great because the contemporary issue is directly related by the prophet to eternal truth ; and thus he leaves to after generations a statement in which the truth endures even when the circumstances which gave him his vision of it have been forgotten.   But Blake, writing in emulation of him, reads mystic symbolism into every reference to Moab, or Israel, or Philistia, and for fear his own vision of truth should fail by reason of its transparency, invents a counter-array of names in order to secure sublimity to it by making it unintelligible. One further point deserves attention.   The true pro-phecy has its birth at a time of national stress and voices the needs or aspiration of a people.   Some of Blake's earlier prophetical writing is thus occasioned, as by the War of American Independence and the Revo-lution in France, and there is no doubt that these

events were fundamental influences in his life. But he
does not bring his vision into a vital relation with them ;
and in the later works, the *Milton* and *Jerusalem*, the
material occasion is often supremely trivial. Mr. E.
J. Ellis, one of the most enthusiastic exponents of
Blake's mystical system, gives it as his opinion that
Blake destroyed ten out of the twelve books of his
Milton, because, in a wave of gratitude and generous
feeling, he recognised that the quarrel between himself
and Hayley—which was the theme of the prophecy—
was represented in them unfairly.

Blake had an unusually powerful mind, and whenever we see him exercising it on the normal material of
life, we feel no doubt of its integrity. Doubt arises
only as regards that part of his experience in which he
leaves common humanity behind him. He claims to
be in direct touch with a certain profound aspect of
reality, to which the natural man can have no access.
A certain scheme of life, a certain mystical interpretation of the meaning of life, hovered consistently
before his eyes and all his utterances bear upon it.
But schematic consistency is not among the attributes
of a true poetic vision. Systematisation is essentially
the task of an inferior mental apparatus. Vision
implies an object ; and the object which Blake believed
to have been brought before him was the spiritual

nature of the universe. Glimpses of , this spiritual
nature have been the inspiration of poets in all ages,
and a certain divine *inconsistency* appears in the account
of what they have seen, witnessing to the transcendent
nature of the vision. Ask for the systematisation of
those glimpses and you will find no answer except in
the entire history of philosophic thought. Look at a
flower, you do not see system ; you see life and beauty ;
the system it will tax a generation of botanists to
reveal. Blake, looking at the ultimate manifestation
of beauty and of life, believed and passionately proclaimed that he saw not life only, but system also. In
believing that private quarrels could be a proper
medium for the conveyance of eternal truth he committed a parallel mistake. In the first he denied
poetry, in the second prophecy. And thus he was
guilty of self-deception touching the very things that
were dearest to his heart ; self-deception so convincing
that it still transmits itself to many of his readers. It
was a mental obsession by which his whole life—that
wonderful intensely glowing life of his—was coloured.
It was a kind of madness.

CHAPTER V

BLAKE'S THEORY OF THE IMAGINATION

THE splendid fire and fervour of Blake's utterance are qualities which make him a dangerous subject for criticism. There can be no criticism worth the name but what is based on sympathy and appreciation. And to sympathise with Blake is to be swept along by him, to be devoured by his flames and shot heavenward, forgetful that one is but common fuel momentarily transmuted into a spark. "Shall painting be confined to the sordid drudgery of fac-simile representations of merely mortal and perishing substances and not be, as poetry and music are, elevated to its own proper sphere of invention and visionary conception? No, it shall not be so! Painting, as well as poetry and music, exists and exults in immortal thoughts." "I assert, for myself, that I do not behold the outward creation, and that to me it is hindrance and not action. 'What!' it will be questioned, 'when the sun rises do you not see a round

disc of fire, somewhat like a guinea?' Oh! no, no!
I see an innumerable company of the heavenly host,
crying: 'Holy, holy, holy, is the Lord God
Almighty!'" "I feel that a Man may be happy in
this world, and I know that this world is a World
of Imagination and Vision. I see everything I paint
in this World: but everybody does not see alike. To
the eyes of a miser a Guinea is more beautiful than
the Sun, and a bag worn with the use of money has
more beautiful proportions than a Vine filled with
grapes. The tree which moves some to tears of joy is
in the eyes of others only a Green thing that stands in
the way. Some see Nature all Ridicule and Deformity,
and by these I shall not regulate my proportions;
and some scarce see Nature at all. But to the eyes
of the Man of Imagination Nature is Imagination
itself." The burning heat which glows behind these
words carries with it the conviction that they are
the statement of some great truth. It is hardly possible not to be carried away by them. But to be
carried away by them is to abandon the true standpoint of criticism. For unless the critic, however
whole-hearted his initial sympathy, is able to recover
his equilibrium and give his verdict in the sobriety
that comes of detachment, he has mistaken his voca-
tion.

Blake's theory of the imagination is one of the chief corner-stones of his system. Every one recognises him now as the forerunner of Wordsworth, Coleridge, Shelley and Keats, and the romantic poetry of freedom and of passion which they inaugurated. "When Blake spoke the first word of the nineteenth century," says Mr. Arthur Symons, "there was no one to hear it; and now that his message, the message of emancipation from reality through the 'shaping spirit of imagination' has penetrated the world, and is slowly remaking it, few are conscious of the first utterer in modern times of the message with which all are familiar." If that is so, either Blake's critics or Blake himself are very much to blame. The world has had every opportunity in recent years of familiarising itself with his message and with him; and if he is still unacknowledged, it must be because the precise meaning of his message has never been made clear. I have myself searched diligently for a clear statement of it, and have not as yet been successful in discovering one. Professor Raleigh, it seems to me, has given as delicate and beautiful a statement as possible of what Blake ought to have meant, of what, no doubt, he meant to mean; and perhaps it would be better for the world if it could rest content with that. But I do not think the world is going to rest content with it,

and for this reason : that Professor Raleigh has given
the truth without allowing enough for the qualifications; whereas, in everything that Blake puts out,
whether theory or practice, the qualifications are nine-
tenths of the whole, and must always continue, by
their mere bulk, to obscure the tithe of truth remaining until they are detached from it in full daylight
and deliberately set aside.

Nothing, of course, is simpler and nothing is more
tempting than to feel rapturously sympathetic when
Blake says he sees angels instead of the sunrise.
When first he said it, people thought him a madman
for his pains. Now, as Mr. Symons reminds us, this
" message of emancipation from reality " is " slowly
remaking the world." It becomes therefore a more
than ever imperative duty to decide exactly what
Blake meant by it. After all, is our emancipation
from reality a thing which, even if it were desirable,
could ever come to pass ? Perhaps there can be no
better means of detaching oneself from a statement
made in a moment of fervour and coming to a true
estimate of its bearing and value, than to turn to
some other example of the same or a similar statement made in a moment of calm. It will be remembered that Blake had a habit of calling down contempt
upon the Greeks and upon Greek art, of which he

knew nothing, because, among the Greeks, "Memory
was the Mother of the Muses." It was a harmless myth
enough, and had no metaphysical import: before
writing was invented, music and poetry could only
survive by being learned by heart. But I strongly
suspect that Blake came across the doctrine in a
metaphysical connection as used or rather touched
on by Plato in the *Theœtetus*, and that this was
enough to give him his life-long prejudice. It is in
the same dialogue that Plato, in his quiet way, makes
a statement which Blake was to take up and proclaim
in his most passionate style two thousand years later.
"If any one were to ask you, Theætetus," Socrates
says: "with what does a man see black and white
colours? and with what does he hear high and low
sounds? You would say, if I am not mistaken, 'With
the eyes and with the ears.' 'I should.' 'The free
use of words and phrases, rather than minute precision,
is generally characteristic of a liberal education, and
the opposite is pedantic; but sometimes precision is
necessary, and I believe that the answer which you
have given is open to the charge of incorrectness;
for which is more correct, to say that we see or hear
with the eyes or the ears, or through the eyes and the
ears?' 'I should say "through," Socrates, rather
than " with." ' 'Yes, my boy, for no one can suppose

that in each of us, as in a sort of Trojan horse, there
are perched a number of unconnected senses, which
do not meet in some one nature, the mind.'" Who
that has been caught up by Blake's fervour, can deny
the cooling, tranquillising influence of such a passage
as this? What can be more consoling than to remember that Blake, in the rapturous claim he made
to spiritual vision, was, in one aspect of the matter,
sinking all his contemporaries to the level of "a sort
of Trojan horses," and that his great distinction between seeing with and seeing through the eye was,
according to Plato's understanding, so universally
acceptable that only a pedant would think necessary
to insist upon it? "I question not my corporeal eye
any more than I would question a window concerning a sight; I look through it and not with it."
"Yes, my boy, for no one can say that in each of us,
as in a sort of Trojan horse, there are perched a
number of unconnected senses which do not meet in
one nature, the mind." Such a collocation should
give us a new courage as we launch the frail barque
of criticism upon the tempestuous seas of Blake's
practice and theory.

If Blake's conception of life is to become of any real
value to us, we must discover what it was. Blake, we
know, spoke of Wordsworth, who was the first to give a

*Be calm, my child, remember that you
must do all the good you can the present day*

Published by J. Johnson Sept.r 1 1791.

MARY WOLLSTONECRAFT ILLUSTRATED
BRITISH MUSEUM

To face p. 74

coherent and intelligible account of the modern idea of
the imagination and its place in art, as an atheist.
"I fear Wordsworth loves Nature—and Nature is the
work of the Devil. The Devil is in us, as far as we are
Nature." And again, "Natural objects always did and
now do weaken, deaden, and obliterate imagination in
me. Wordsworth must know that what he writes
valuable is not to be found in Nature." The latter
remark, it is worth remembering, was called forth by
one of Wordsworth's most exalted passages—the well-
known lines beginning, "Wisdom and Spirit of the
Universe!" and proceeding to exquisite description of
the sights and sounds which the poet had loved in boy-
hood. To decide exactly what criticism Blake intended
to advance against it is the more difficult because,
in certain passages, Blake formulates his theory in
language that seems to bring it very close to Wordsworth's. Of these the passage from the letter to Dr.
Trusler, quoted earlier, is by far the most notable. It
contains the whole problem of Blake's theory in a nut-
shell. Blake, it will be seen, speaks here of Nature and
Imagination side by side. Nature, we gather, is a
common material interpreted by different persons differently, according to their different faculties—"For
the eye altering, alters all." And the true view of
Nature, Blake seems to add, is the view of her as she

appears to the Imagination. " To the eye of the Man of
Imagination, Nature is Imagination itself." All this
is straightforward enough and perfectly intelligible.
Difficulty arises, however, because, on the whole, Blake's
statements do not accord with the interpretation I have
just given of the statement he makes here. His normal
attitude is that " Nature is the work of the Devil." Is
there, then, any reconciliation between these two con-
flicting positions to be found ?

Perhaps we may put ourselves very simply on the
track of understanding, by a reflection upon certain
elementary considerations which Blake's description of
the sunrise involves. After all, the main question to be
decided is, in what relation Blake conceived the imagination to stand to other mental processes. His reply
would probably be that it includes all others, and
supersedes them. But I think we shall find that this is
a point of view which he states in words merely ; he
does not succeed in making any consistent application of
the theory in his normal thinking or in his work. To
bring out my meaning I shall be forced to descend to a
consideration of " minute particulars," but this is a
process to which Blake, of all people, would have been
the last to take exception. It will be observed at once,
then, that Blake's description of the rising sun as " a
round disc of fire, somewhat like a guinea," is a pretty

piece of evidence, were any such evidence needed, that
he could, when he chose, see through the corporeal
eye as clearly as any one; and that his statement,
" for myself, I do not behold the outward creation,"
means no more than that conscious study of natural
forms had ceased to be a part of his artistic or spiritual
activity. What still remains to be discovered, however,
is the connection between the sunrise and the heavenly
host. If Nature is the work of the Devil, if natural
objects weaken and deaden imagination, how comes it
to pass that the appearance of this round, guinea-shaped
disc can produce so marvellous a vision? Nothing, of
course, is easier than to save Blake's position, as most
of his critics are willing to do, by tossing off a few vague
and magnanimous remarks. That method, however,
can give no permanent satisfaction. It cannot be too
emphatically pointed out that Blake was formulating a
theory; and the fact that he was a poet and an artist is
not to be adduced in extenuation of his theories, when
he unwisely stoops to become a theoriser. We have to
consider in the most prosaic manner possible whether
they hold water. Another example may be of service
in enabling us precisely to emphasise the point at issue.
It was while quite a child, says Gilchrist, that Blake
had his first vision. " Sauntering along, the boy looks
up and sees a tree filled with angels, bright angelic

wings bespangling every bough like stars." Vision and
imagination are used by Blake, it need not be said, as
convertible terms ; and the problem which faces us—it
is much like a desecration to handle it ; but there can
be no escape for us ; we are obliged to do so—is to
determine, as it were, from the side of the object what
is the relation of the angels to the tree. It has been
suggested with much likelihood that the tree may have
been a fruit tree white with bloom : clearly there is
nothing in such a suggestion that touches the essentials
of the case, or helps us more than a very little towards
a solution of our problem. But, again, " The tree
which moves some to tears of joy is in the eyes of others
only a green thing that stands in the way." Here the
problem intensifies. Do the tears of joy arise from a
vision of the tree as a tree—does the man of Imagination weep for the wonderful beauty of which the tree
itself is a revelation to him ; or because he sees no tree
at all, not so much even as a green thing standing in
his way, but puts an angel there instead ?

We may emphasise the necessity of working this
matter out by quoting a few sentences more from Mr.
Symons's able critique. "Blake is the only poet who
sees all temporal things under the form of eternity. To
him reality is merely a symbol, and he catches at its
terms, hastily and faultily, as he catches at the lines of

the drawing-master, to represent, as in a faint image, the clear and shining outlines of what he sees with the imagination : through the eye, not with it, as he says. . . . For the most part, he is just conscious that what he sees as ' an old man grey ' is no more than a ' frowning thistle ' :

> ' For double the vision my eyes do see,
>   And a double vision is always with me.
>   With my inward eye, 'tis an old man grey,
>   With my outward, a thistle across my way.'

In being so far conscious," adds Mr. Symons, "he is only recognising the symbol, not admitting the reality." I must confess that Mr. Symons's illustration seems to me a particularly unhappy one. If Blake hastily and faultily catches at a thistle, in order, as in a faint image, to represent the clear and shining outlines of a grey old man, I do not see why, in so doing, he can claim to be seeing temporal things under the form of eternity. Thistles and old men are, after all, equally mere symbols, and it does not argue any great poetic insight to confuse the two. It will be worth while to examine rather more closely the poem in which these lines occur, in order to get a complete idea of the mental attitude which they presuppose. They would appear to have been written in the late summer of the year 1801, rather less than a

year after Blake's arrival in Felpham. Before returning
to London he was to remain at Felpham two years more,
but the whole problem of his position is already clearly
before him. He states it forcibly in a letter to Butts,
written some six months later : "I find on all hands
great objections to my doing anything but the mere
drudgery of business, and intimations that if I do not
confine myself to this I shall not live. This has always
pursued me. . . . This from Johnson and Fuseli brought
me down here, and this from Mr. Hayley will bring me
back again. . . . If we fear to do the dictates of our
angels, and tremble at the tasks set before us . . . who
can describe the dismal torments of such a state ? I
too well remember the threats I heard! 'If you, who
are organised by Divine Providence for spiritual communion, refuse, and bury your talent in the earth, even
though you should want actual bread, sorrow and
desperation pursue you through life, and after death,
shame, and confusion of face, to eternity.' " The poem,
we may suppose, was written at the time when those
threats were first making themselves heard. Blake has
set out, on an exquisite summer morning, to walk from
Felpham to Lavant. He is in a state of the greatest
mental tumult. He is determining to leave Felpham
and return to London, and the various considerations,
that urge him this way and that, are symbolised to him,

or personified, in the sweet influence of the morning air,
in the divine loveliness of Nature, and in the forms of
angels, demons, friends and relatives; he leaves it quite
uncertain—and I doubt whether any two Blake-students
would agree—which argue which way; but at last the
controversy is focussed in the form of a frowning thistle
which stands before him on his path. With the inward
eye he sees it as an old man grey; and from the mouth
of the old man issue dismal threats, warning him of the
misery in store for him, the contempt which will be
visited on him by his friends, if he carries out his intention. The horror and disgust of it all surge through
his mind.

> I struck the thistle with my foot,
> And broke him up from his delving root.
> ' Must the duties of life each other cross?
> Must every joy be dung and dross?
> Must my dear Butts feel cold neglect
> Because I give Hayley his due respect? . . .
> The curses of Los, the terrible shade,
> And his dismal terrors make me afraid.'
> So I spoke, and struck in my wrath
> The old man weltering upon my path.

This, however, is only the prologue to a far fiercer
agony of strife. The sun himself appears before Blake
in the form of Los; not, however, as Los the Spirit of

F

Prophecy, but Los the "terrible shade," lord of the natural corporeal life. Blake defies the apparition, and triumphantly asserts his independence of all temporal cares. Immediately the whole material universe seems to melt before him in the glow and glory of his inspiration.

The splendid impetuosity of Blake's character is hardly anywhere revealed more convincingly than at the climax of this poem. But equally from the poetic or mystic or visionary point of view, the episode of the thistle seems to my mind, as Blake himself gives warning it is likely to do, trivial and unworthy; and the triviality of it has, I think, only escaped attention because of the extreme obscurity of the context in which it appears. What possible value can there be in the imaginative realm which Blake would introduce us to, unless we can rely on finding there something at least approximately the equivalent of what in this "vegetable world" we call a sense of decency, or relativity, or proportion? Grant that because Blake's mind is in turmoil he has the right to see the bitterness of his grievance concentrated in the form of a thistle which he chances to meet when he is out walking; what is the spiritual value of the so-called double vision which enables him to transmute this thistle into a hoary-headed old man, beyond the added sting of scorn it gives to the violence with which he strikes and defaces it? It seems to me obvious that no real gain comes of the transmutation, and that if we are to explain it we must consider the incident, not poetically, but simply as exemplifying Blake's normal mental habit. He speaks in this way of the thistle, not in order to summon up a concrete image of a spiritual event, but because the incident he describes, the transmutation he describes, actually took place. He actually spurned a thistle from his path, picturing it to himself as an old man as he did so, and presenting the act to himself as one which had a deep significance in his inner life. As Mr. Symons points out, the thistle, as a thistle, was not real to him. Nothing was real to him except what, if he were a normal man, we should call his private concerns. He considers them to be of world-moving importance; so much hinges upon his decision, whether to remain at Felpham, or whether to return to London, that the universe itself is a mere pawn in the struggle, and dissolves when his resolution is made. And he sees this dissolution of the universe, consequent upon the destruction of a wayside thistle, as a notable event in his mind's history, a great imaginative act.

There might have been some greatness in it if he had left it at that; if, having made his resolution, he had proceeded deliberately to carry it out. But this same struggle continues to be the centre of his spiritual life for two years more, and is made the subject of two of his longest and least intelligible writings—writings in which, though confessedly autobiographical, the characters and machinery are on a scale that would suggest some wide world-tragedy, in which, as on this earlier walk of his, the universe is represented as waiting and watching while Blake uproots a thistle. "I may praise it," he says, speaking probably of the more elaborate of the two, "since I dare not pretend to be any other than the secretary; the authors are in eternity. I consider it as the grandest poem that this world contains." I do not think there can be any doubt, for a reader who is prepared to examine these facts judicially, that the prospect of "emancipation from reality," of which Mr. Symons takes them for a pledge, is one which they can give him no warrant for accepting. Reality, as I hinted, is not to be shaken off so easily. Indeed, all art, all criticism presuppose it, the only difficulty being to discover what it is. Mr. Symons himself, who speaks in one sentence of reality as "merely a symbol," speaks in the next of "the unchanging realities of the imagination." Reality, after all, is truth; and even when the reality is imaginative, it is unchanging. The old bondage attaches to it still. If it is the fault of the thistle that it remains always a thistle, the same fault, it would appear, attaches also to the old man I arbitrarily put in its place. He, too, if he is real, is unchanging, and all that I have to decide is whether I prefer to bind myself to the thistle or to him. If I see angels when the sun comes up, the angels, perhaps, are better than the sun; but that will depend, as Blake himself would say, upon the eye that sees them; many would prefer to see a sunrise with Turner rather than with Blake, and would find its reality not less unchanging in eternal, and far less monotonous in temporal, aspects; while the use of the imagination, though it would operate differently in each case, would be equally essential in either.

The more I relate this poem to the conditions in which it was actually conceived by Blake, relate it, that is, to the leading events of his life before and after its composition, the more I am inclined to believe, what many other of Blake's statements render likely, that he used the word "imagination" in at least two completely different senses, though without being himself aware that he did so. To get a right judgment of Blake's theory of the imagination and of the practical method he based on it, it is, I believe, necessary to recognise that on this subject, a subject of the most

vital consequence to him both in thought and life, he
fell into a quite elementary confusion. Happily, in a
letter to Butts, he has given what seems to me the
clearest evidence of this confusion, but given it with
an innocence so childlike that none of his commentators,
so far as I am aware, have seen the significance of it or
connected it with his profounder or more impassioned
statements.   I refer to the following words: "I can
soon send some of your designs which I have nearly
completed.   In the meantime, by my sister's hands, I
transmit to Mrs. Butts an attempt at your likeness,
which I hope she who is the best judge will think like.
. . . Next time I have the happiness to see you, I am
determined to paint another portrait of you from life in
my best manner, for memory will not do in such minute
operations; for I have now discovered that without
nature before the painter's eye, he can never produce
anything in the walks of natural painting.   Historical
designing is one thing, and portrait painting another;
and they are as distinct as any two arts can be.   Happy
would that man be who could unite them!" This is
indeed a portentous discovery for the great advocate of
imaginative painting to have made, and his announcement of the truth as news shows decisively that it has
escaped him hitherto.   Having been a year at Felpham,
he sets to work to produce a miniature portrait of Mr.

Butts, his patron, whom he has not seen since leaving London : he is amazed to find that the resultant likeness proves unsatisfactory. But " he who does not imagine in stronger and better lineaments and in stronger and better light than his perishing and mortal eye can see does not imagine at all. The painter of this work asserts that all his imaginations appear to him infinitely more perfect and more minutely organised than anything seen by his mortal eye." Imagination, as Blake says, has nothing to do with memory : but, like many of his sayings, this is a saying and nothing more. It is one thing, certainly, to draw an imaginary head, another to imagine a true likeness of a familiar face. But so far Blake himself had failed to discover where the difference lay. It is clear that he must have had a colossal power of visual memory ; equally clear that we must be prepared to find astounding gaps in the artistic theories he so passionately asserts. We find in practice that minute organisation, so far as it is introduced by Blake into his designs, is generally superinduced, and destructive of their perfection. In proportion as he organises, he loses power. But he believed that the persons in his historical designs were clearer to him in their individuality than the " vegetative " features of his mortal friends. He was mistaken.

The unsuccessful effort to paint Butts from memory

on the one side, the consequent discovery that there
was a difference between calling up the image of an
individual known in experience and conceiving the
image of a never-observed historical event, the naïve
recognition that it might be a conceivable aim in the
development of the art of painting to set the purely
internal and the purely external processes in combination—all this shows, as I said earlier, that Blake, while
worshipping the imaginative functions of the artist, had
not familiarised himself with certain elementary distinc-
tions in our use of the word imagination itself; and he
was probably further confused by the fact that, being
himself poet as well as painter, his own imaginative
gift flowed in two separate channels.   By imagination
we mean, according to its simplest sense, the power to
raise before the mind images of things not at the
moment presented to it by the senses ; the images are not
necessarily to be conceived as visual : imagination may
be of sounds or indeed of any experiences whatever.
But to understand the immense importance of the part
which imagination plays even in the most unassuming
of lives, we must remember that its power is not limited
to the recovery of our sense impressions in the order in
which we originally received them.   We early derive
from our impressions the unanalysed conception of
experience as an ordered system, and therefore we have

only to assume one fact as true to see that the truth of
it will involve determined consequences on this side and
on that. The power to follow out these consequences,
to elaborate a real scheme of co-ordinate experiences
following from or leading up to the fact which we take
as our hypothesis, is essentially the imaginative power.
It is familiar to us in its application to artistic work ;
but that is, in reality, only one of the many spheres in
which it operates, and the whole fabric of our social
life, the entire possibility of further social development,
depend on it. The individual's capacity to become in
any true sense the member of a society is conditioned
by his power to see the common social medium, not
only directly through his own eyes, but indirectly also as
it appears to the eyes of others whose circumstances are
not the same as his. " If I were situated in B's place,"
he must be able to say to himself, " and possessed B's
faculties and feelings, how would this arrangement or
proposal or ideal present itself to my mind ? " To this
faculty, clearly, in its common human application no
limit can be set, and there is no question but it
is the same faculty as that which when it operates
artistically we call the imagination. That it is the
same seems likely from the fact that artists as a class,
concentrating, as they are apt to do, their imaginative
faculty upon their work, and no doubt coming to

associate the use of it with what we may call immaterial issues, are notoriously unsocial, notoriously incapable of accommodating themselves pleasantly to the conveniences of their neighbours. They have specialised the imaginative power and overtaxed it. Blake, we must add, in spite of his greatness, is a signal instance of the most exclusive specialisation one can conceive. To read *An Island in the Moon* and the Notes on Reynolds's Discourses, to reflect upon Blake's attitude to Flaxman, Hayley, Stothard, even Cromek, is to realise that you are face to face with a man who, for the faculty of social imagination, shows a blank. There is a detestable epigram in his note-book to the effect that

> The only man I ever knew
> Who did not almost make me spue
> Is Fuseli, &c.

and his supporters have perhaps found means to explain it in a mystical sense. To a dispassionate view, his attitude to friends and acquaintances in everyday life explains it quite sufficiently.

The employment of the faculty in its normal artistic application is so much before the world in the writings of æsthetic critics and elsewhere that it seems scarcely necessary to exemplify it. Every artistic production involves the combining of impressions in an order in which they never could be found combined in the common life of every day; it involves the selection of some, the rejection of others, and the accommodation of all to the particular artistic medium in which they are to be expressed. All these processes have their value according to the degree in which they can rightly be called imaginative; in so far, that is, as the artist chooses, modifies, rejects, because he is for the time living and feeling within the limits of the ideal conception on which, with its realisation in a form appropriate to it, depends the significance of his work. Some conceptions, together with the media through which they find expression, are of course far more widely removed than others from the normal experiences of life; and it is to these— the *Ancient Mariner* may be quoted as the best-known example of them—that we are accustomed to turn for the most conspicuous examples of the artistic imaginative effort. It ought to be remembered, on the other hand, that the removal to an unfamiliar world, though the imagination may be taxed to reach it, sets the imagination on its arrival wonderfully free. If you take on the burden of strangeness, you put off the burden of complexity; and it may be questioned whether the most exalted exercise of

artistic imagination is not rather to be looked for in
the treatment of human life in its familiar conditions.

This reflection may lead us to an understanding of
the nature of a different kind of imaginative effort, of
a kind of effort, that is, which, though called imaginative, seems to occupy itself quite differently and to
issue in quite different results. It will be remembered
that imagination, according to the theory formulated,
for example, by Wordsworth, has for one of its central
functions—not, what we have been so far assuming,
the summoning to the mind of images not actually
presented to it by the senses—but the more distinctive,
more fundamental apprehension of those images which
the senses do actually present. Imagination is in this
sense the power which would seem to stand behind
our everyday processes of observation, ready to rein-
force them. And its reinforcement has the effect, not
of withdrawing us from the common objects which our
senses perceive, but of introducing us to a far deeper,
far more intimate communion with them. To see
completely this chair, house, village, mountain, sunrise, is only possible for him who can raise his sensuous
impression of them to an imaginative power. And the
object is, in effect, thus raised by an action of the mind
which provides for it such a context as the mere sense
impression has not of itself the means of summoning

up. There are as it were images which the mind must draw from its resources and add to the sensuous image actually before it. To find them, to make them live, to combine them in their true relation with the object and with one another—these and other mental processes involved, too numerous and subtle for analysis, are rightly called imaginative processes; and the total act that issues in this fuller vision is strictly speaking an imaginative act. Imagination is, in fact, the key to all complete experience. Setting aside that aspect of our consciousness in which it appears as receptivity, viewing it as an active force, you may say that its essential function is the imagination.

But is this what Blake, in his enthusiastic advocacy, wished to claim for it? For myself, I feel quite confident that it was not so. Because Blake was a mystic and a poet, he was in the habit of making free use of metaphorical language. It is a danger of metaphorical language that, in the very nature of it, it must allow a certain freedom of interpretation; it postulates a sympathetic listener. But nothing could be more mistaken than to suppose on that account that in any great writer metaphors are used to cover confusion or vagueness of thought. Blake's life was spent in calling witness to the paramount claims of the imagination over every other form of human activity. He believed his message must be as clear to others as it was convincing to himself.

> Trembling I sit, day and night. My friends are
>   astonished at me :
> Yet they forgive my wanderings.   I rest not from my
>   great task :
> To open the eternal worlds !   To open the immortal
>   eyes
> Of man inwards; into the worlds of thought: into
>   eternity
> Ever expanding in the bosom of God, the human
>   imagination.

I think it must be clear from this and many other passages that, to Blake's idea, the true exercise of the imagination involved, not merely a metaphorical, but an actual and total, rejection of the world revealed to us by our senses, and a substitution for images of things, as we perceive them sensuously, of other images perceived by the unaided mind.   The most fundamental of his instincts was that instinct of the mystic which, beginning, as he began, with the discovery of the infinite in all things, is liable to end, as he ended, with a contempt for the finite on the mere ground that the infinite is not contained in it.   And so, aspiring after a more immediate communion than the " vegetative " conditions of our existence seemed naturally to afford, he believed that he had found the secret of it in a complete withdrawal which should leave him free to concentrate his whole attention upon the revelations of his "inward vision." There are many evidences to show that the process by which he developed this inward vision was one that did violence to his nature; and there is little or nothing in the transcript of his visionary experiences which marks them as in any sense the vehicles of a deeper or a clearer truth than a mind as sensitive and powerful as Blake's must have reached by the study of the external world. Blake, as we saw, had, to set out with, a very highly developed power of imaginative visualisation; he could recall to mind the shape and appearance of things he had seen with wonderful precision. This is the imagination of the artist in its simplest form, that is, as associated with memory. But "imagination," says Blake, "has nothing to do with memory." He was, of course, mistaken; it has much to do with it. He meant, however, to convey that the imaginative power, in its application to the tasks of artistic conception and design, did not proceed in any conscious reference to the materials amassed in previous experiences. He rightly saw the essence of it as the entering into and creation of a new experience. But he seemed not to have grasped the obvious fact that experience is a ladder, to be mounted one rung at a time, and that the nature of every new step you take must be conditioned by the nature of those you have taken already. No more convincing example of this need be looked for than his own designs. The creative instinct is everywhere in them to be seen propped on the crutches of memory; and it is, of course, the arbitrary limits Blake has imposed on his experience which has crippled him. For half his memories are memories of himself.

Moreover, and here I think we reach the heart of the matter, he seemed to suppose that the mere fact that an image presented itself to "inward" and not to "outward" vision gave it all the validity, trustworthiness, and eternal truth and glory which he worshipped as belonging to the works of the imagination alone. In short, he failed to distinguish between the visualising and the creative imagination. His power of visualisation was so abnormal that he became unconsciously its slave. To use his own expression—and the inchoate vagueness of a multitude of his drawings will testify at once to the accuracy of it—he *copied* from Imagination, and the imagination he copied from was a thing which, because he worshipped it, he had ceased to think necessary to guide or to control. Mr. Symons tells an admirable story which brings the whole truth home. " I was once showing Rodin some facsimiles of Blake's

drawings, and telling him about Blake. I said : ' He
used to literally see these figures : they are not mere
inventions.' ' Yes,' said Rodin, ' he saw them once ;
he should have seen them three or four times.'" This
beautiful beam of sanity from M. Rodin operates
among Blake's hot-headed theorisings with an effect
almost equivalent to that of the remark I earlier
quoted of Plato from the *Theœtetus*. The fact is
that artistic invention and the fruit of it have
very little in common with the impulse to day-
dreaming, and to copy your dreams is as much a matter
of "sordid drudgery" as to copy nature. Blake failed
to recognise this, and the failure involved him in the
inability to distinguish between an invention and a
dream. He never tires indeed of insisting upon the
minutest articulation of parts as an essential feature of
imaginative vision : "I entreat that the spectator will
attend to the hands and feet ; to the lineaments of the
countenance : they are all descriptive of character, and
not a line is drawn without intention, and that most
discriminate and particular ; " but his work does not as
a whole exemplify this claim convincingly. In how
many of his drawings is a unified conception so clearly
grasped and held as to be able to express itself not
only in the main lines of intention but in fully organised
and duly subordinated detail ? It is common even in

so considered a work as the *Illustrations to the book of Job* to see passages marked by crudity and shapelessness on the one hand—passages in which the imagination has failed to come to a complete understanding with itself —and on the other, passages—and these are probably the more numerous—on which the imagination has been allowed to play disproportionately, that is, in isolation, producing an artificial, what in a work of art we may rightly call an unimaginative, intricacy of detail. Of course, the true judgment of Blake can never be delivered by comparing his forms and figures with a conventional realistic standard ; they can only be judged in relation to their imaginative aim ; but where they fail, the failure will always be, as M. Rodin points out, an imaginative failure. It is not that there is too much imagination in them, but that there is too little.

Blake's intellectual self-contradictions, arising partly from the versatility of his genius, partly from the deplorable narrowness of outlook that characterised the period he lived in, partly from a still more deplorable arrogance in himself which made it impossible for him, by modifying his own ideas, to meet the ideas of others, will not be seen in their true light until they are related to the deep spiritual insight and integrity which seems to justify and almost to explain them, though it can indeed never explain them away. The imagination, of which in its practical uses he discoursed so confusingly, was conceived by him and existed in him as the faculty by which man is able in this as in all ages to "walk with God." It was the central aim of Blake's life so to walk. In his early years he saw God in nature, and the communion with Nature was to him as to all great artists a communion with the Divine. But, later, the mystic craving for a more immediate revelation grew in him, and led him to cast aside the works of God as a hindrance to the purer vision. That purer vision, the vision by which man, rising above, forsaking the world of sense, sees himself transfigured, and discovers that the ultimate secret of his life is the identity of the Divine and Human natures, was the source in him of a perpetually recurring inspiration. " I am not ashamed, afraid, or averse to tell you what ought to be told," he writes to his patron Butts, " that I am under the direction of messengers from heaven, daily and nightly." In nothing that I have said earlier has it been my wish to throw doubt upon the beauty or even upon the sublimity of Blake's religious aspiration. But I cannot question that he misinterpreted the nature of what he believed to be the revelations he obtained as a response to it. He began life as a great artist, and with his greatness as an artist he might have united, as he wished to unite it, the greatness of a mystic also. Difficulties arose for him because he attempted to reconcile these divergent impulses externally; it was not enough for him to be an artist and a mystic, he desired also to be a philosopher. And this desire, on which he himself perpetually called down his most terrific imprecations, came near to be his undoing. For the methods of art and mysticism are not philosophically reconcilable, and no violence of asseveration to the contrary can ever make them so. Blake tried it. There was an early period of his life in which the two-fold instinct—the artistic vision, the mystical translation—could express themselves in him without any sense of a division between them—the period which produced among others the exquisite designs and imagery of the *Book of Thel*:

> Art thou a worm? Image of weakness, art thou but
>   a worm?
> I see thee like an infant wrappèd in the Lily's leaf.

But in the attempt to pursue and to assert an underlying principle of unity, he only so far succeeded as to assert the vaguer principle of which mysticism is the issue. And having asserted it, having thus allowed his " Spectre" of reason to meddle with the deeper in-

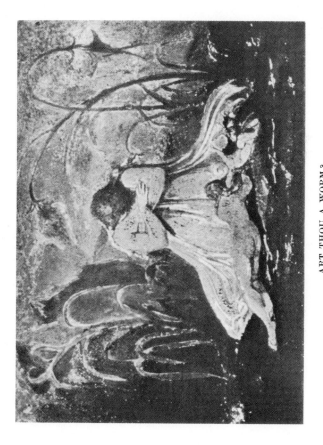

ART THOU A WORM?
BRITISH MUSEUM

To face p. 100

stincts of his life, he was driven, by the very passion of his own utterances, to a denial of the more complex, more organic principle which issues in the artistic ideal. He remained an artist, and the artistic impulses remained operative within him; but he had deprived them of their true source of nourishment; and they therefore turned in hunger on the one source of life remaining to them, the mystic consciousness itself; and here, inevitably, they produced the turmoil and confusion with which, in its various expressions, the world has grown so familiar—Blake's so-called Prophetic Books. The agony, the wrestlings, the confusion of soul which pervade the *Milton* and the *Jerusalem* are not to be explained as springing from a contest with any external foe. It is an internal warfare which they reveal; we see the spirit of the artist fettered—bound by a too narrow philosophy to the pursuit of a mystical abstraction;—unable to find its natural satisfaction in such a pursuit, it projects itself into the mystic consciousness, to build there, out of the rejected ruins of the world native to it, unwieldy forms reflective of its perversion and its desire, substituting for the free and happy exercise of purely imaginative activities a categorical and tempestuous assertion of the integrity of the imagination itself.

CHAPTER VI

THE RATIO OF THE FIVE SENSES

ONE of the most interesting parts of Blake's doctrine is that which relates to Perception and the " Five Senses." The subject is one which it would repay us to consider separately, and we shall best introduce it by a handful of representative quotations. It is among the solaces of Blake-criticism that the kernel of his belief on every topic that interested him is always readily discoverable. His beliefs were, so to speak, all kernel, and in his laborious and involved exposition of them he really does little more than repeat the same statements over and over again. He speaks, then, of the senses in one passage as " the chief inlets of Soul in this age "; but the expression is perhaps satirical. In any case, to be understood it must be related to its antithesis:

How do you know but every Bird that cuts the airy
    way
Is an immense world of delight, clos'd by your senses
    five ?

It is on the limitations of sense, as he here metaphorically suggests them, that Blake's emphasis is usually laid. This becomes the subject of one of the rare passages of beauty which rise like oases before the pilgrim lost in the desert of the Prophetic Books.

> Ah ! weak and wide astray ; ah, shut in narrow doleful form !
> Creeping in reptile flesh upon the bosom of the ground !
> The eye of Man, a little narrow orb, clos'd up and dark,
> Scarcely beholding the great light, conversing with the ground.
> The ear, a little shell, in small volutions shutting out
> True harmonies, and comprehending great as very small.
> The nostrils bent down to the earth and clos'd with senseless flesh ;
> The tongue a little moisture fills, a little food it cloys,
> A little sound it utters, and its cries are faintly heard.

Blake is, of course, carried away here by the pathos of his theme a little ; he makes at the close of his threnody the very mistake which he laments at the beginning of it. For if man sees and hears small things

where he might see and hear great, that frailty in him
has really nothing to do with the fact that he has a
small appetite. Had Blake read his *Alice*, he must
have known that littleness is like " muchness," that
there are many different kinds of it. However, the first
six lines of the quotation make his reasoning sufficiently
clear, and he nowhere expresses it more beautifully. To
the conception he here gives of a confined humanity we
have only to relate his theory as to the nature of the
confining influence, and one of the main threads of his
theorising comes clearly into our hands. The confining
influence is in one word, " Reason," otherwise known
to Blake as " The Ratio of the Five Senses." The
worship of Reason Blake recognised everywhere as the
besetting sin of his contemporaries, and the attempt to
form a religion out of the materials with which reason
works evokes his fiercest and most scornful antagonism.
One of the sections of his *Jerusalem* is prefaced by a
scathing attack upon the Deists, and he has also a
small pamphlet, comprising half a dozen aphorisms,
which he entitles, *There is no Natural Religion*,
adding for a motto " The Voice of one crying in the
Wilderness," to witness the intellectual isolation of
its writer.

Blake's deliverances only become intelligible when it
is remembered that, for him as he makes them, they

AN ILLUSTRATED APHORISM
BRITISH MUSEUM
To face p. 105

never lose their immediate relation to the central principle of his life, his religious aspiration and belief. The complexity of experience worried him. As his mind became with age less widely receptive, he grew more and more inclined to fall back upon the religious experience as his one sure hold upon reality, and to deny or disregard with increasing relentlessness whatever would appear to be inconsistent with it. The relation of reason to the senses, and of both to the central truth of life, he condenses in another small pamphlet; and as in understanding it we understand all Blake has to say upon the subject, it will repay us to set it down entire.

I. Man's perceptions are not bounded by organs of perception; he perceives more than sense (though ever so acute) can discover. II. Reason, or the ratio of all we have already known, is not the same as it shall be when we know more. III. From a perception of only three senses, or three elements, none could deduce a fourth or a fifth. IV. None could have other than natural or organic thoughts if he had none but organic perceptions. V. Man's desires are limited by his perceptions; none can desire what he has not perceived. VI. The desires and perceptions of man untaught by anything but organs of sense, must be limited to objects of sense. Therefore (this in a new style of writing twice the size of what goes before, and all embroidered with flourishes of

ecstasy) God becomes as we are that we may be as
He is.

This is all highly characteristic ; so trenchant and so
true ; so convincing in manner ; so logical in form ; but
in matter, when we come to a final consideration of it,
so full of illogicality and confusion. All depends
on the meaning we can attach to the first aphorism ;
and, luckily, we are aided in this by the existence
of two more aphorisms that deal with the same
subject.

I. Man cannot naturally perceive, but through his
natural or bodily organs. II. Man by his reasoning
power can only compare and judge of what he has
already perceived.

In saying, therefore, that man perceives more
than sense can discover, Blake means to imply
that man has a power of spiritual perception which
brings him into touch with a world of experience
wider than the familiar world of sights and
sounds. He goes on to show rightly that the
function of reason is to introduce method into
experiences already acquired, and that its exercise
is limited to the materials with which perception has
provided it. As experience enlarges there will be more

materials to be arranged and the general effect of the
arrangement will undergo constant modification and
change. So far so good. But remembering that for
Blake reason " is the ratio of the five senses," we must
be prepared to find him excluding altogether from its
operation the materials provided by the power of
spiritual perception—the " more " of which Aphorism I.
makes mention. He offers no ground at all for such an
exclusion ; neither is any ground discoverable for it. It
is a piece of dogma on his part ; it is his fundamental
fallacy. However, he proceeds in the Third Aphorism
to confuse himself still further by an isolated statement,
which does not become less gratuitous because it may
be true. If you had only three senses, he says, and in
consequence could only perceive three kinds of qualities
in objects, you could not by any process of reasoning
provide yourself with another sense, or enlarge the
content of your experience : reason gives you nothing
that you have not got already. The Fourth Aphorism
states a truism of another kind ; to understand it we
must revert to the distinction Blake set up at the start.
He postulated there two kinds of perception, natural
and spiritual ; here he postulates two kinds of thought
to correspond with them. But, says he, if there were
but one kind of perception, the natural, there could be
but one kind of thought—and the spiritual life would

be an illusion. The next two aphorisms contribute the
idea that desire is consequent upon perception : a very
questionable idea at the best. You could not, indeed,
want a banana without first knowing what a banana
was ; but hunger does not arise in a newborn baby
because it has perceived food. However, the triumphant conclusion shows what Blake is aiming at.
Man's desire is for the spiritual life ; he could not
have this desire unless he knew what the spiritual life
was, and he could not know what it was unless he had
perceived it. He has perceived it ; God has revealed it
to him. The human nature is in touch with the
Divine.

What is chiefly of importance to point out in all
this is that so far as Blake attempts to make a philosophical or logical statement, or to construct a chain of
argument, he fails. He has given already in his opening aphorism the only statement which he really needs
for his conclusion ; and as for the darker problems
which it would be of value to clear up, such as the
relation of natural perception to spiritual, the question
whether any such thing as purely "natural" perception
exists, and if so what it is and what spiritual perception is, and why spiritual knowledge is excluded from
the domain of reason ; as for all these problems, which
are implied in his argument, and which, remaining

problems, make it nugatory, he does not so much as see
that they exist.   He himself, when writing as a poet,
breaks down the very division which he is here, as
philosopher, attempting to set up.   "I asked the
prophet Isaiah how he dared so roundly to assert that
God spake to him," and Isaiah answered, "I saw no
God nor heard any in a finite organical perception,
but my *senses discovered the infinite in every thing !* "
and the same mental attitude inspires the beautiful
characteristic quatrain :

> To see a world in a grain of sand
> And a heaven in a wild-flower ;
> Hold infinity in the palm of your hand
> And eternity in an hour.

The fact is that Blake when he thus uses the instinctive language of poetry comes much nearer the just
statement of philosophic truth : and when he philoso-
phises he destroys the very source of his inspiration.
For, of course, the only true perception is that in which
the natural and spiritual are combined, the perception
Blake attributes to Isaiah which discovers the infinite
in everything ; for which, in fact, the distinction between
natural and spiritual disappears.   "For man has closed
himself up till he sees all things through narrow chinks
of his cavern."   "If the doors of perception were

cleansed, everything would appear to man as it is, infinite."

The philosophic thought current in Blake's day left the main facts of life, as Blake understood them, almost unrecognised; its method was too precise for easy accommodation of the infinite. Blake did good service in calling attention to a serious oversight. But his method of criticism was as faulty and one-sided as the method criticised. What was needed was an enlarged idea of the nature of perception and of the world revealed by it, an extension of the domain of reason, a subtler and profounder analysis of the experience it explained and presupposed. Blake's error was to accept the arbitrary limitations within which he found reason and perception working as if no freer working of them were conceivable, and to hurl his anathemas not upon the method, but upon the instruments themselves. And thus his ultimate word both about reason and sense is a word of scorn and of denial. For reason he never had a good word to say; it marked a limit, was " the outward bound and circumference of energy " at its best. But reason after all was a thing which, as an artist, he had no call to concern himself with. It was in his connection of reason with sense, it was when the senses became mere senses to him, that he began to touch on dangerous ground:

How do you know but every bird that cuts the airy
way
Is an immense world of delight, *clos'd* by your senses
five ?

The fascination of that question grew on him, and led
him at last to the greatest calamity that can befall an
artist, the answering it in the affirmative.

CHAPTER VII

BLAKE'S THEORIES OF HIS ART

BLAKE's theory of Art was, like most of his theories, extremely simple. Briefly, the whole of art came, in his eyes, from one source and from one source only. True artistic work could only be done "in the Spirit." " Art is Inspiration. When Michael Angelo or Raphael in their day, or Mr. Flaxman does any of his fine things, he does them in the Spirit," he told Crabb Robinson in his decline, and years previously he had written to Butts, " You will be tempted to think that, as I improve, the pictures, etc., that I did for you are not what I would now wish them to be. On this I beg to say that they are what I intended them, and that I know I never shall do better; for, if I were to do them over again, they would lose as much as they gained, because they were done in the heat of my spirits." An artist's first duty was to acquire the requisite technical dexterity, to learn the language of art : this done, Inspiration spontaneously dictated to him the method of execution appropriate to his designs. Blake, as usual, states with force and intensity the central core of truth, and, as usual, commits the error of supposing that the truth is made up of core and nothing else. It is a condition of all true artistic work that it should be done in the heat of a man's spirits : and no advance in manual dexterity could atone for loss of vitalising power. But all the work that men do in the heat of their spirits is not art. Some of the worst things that ever have been done have been done in that state of unreflecting rapture, which is a condition of artistic work ; nor does it follow, even though a man have the faculties and the trained dexterity of the artist, that his rapture will not at times betray him. To appreciate Blake's theories both for what they were and for what they failed to be, we must bear in mind that they left him no means of distinguishing between a true and a spurious inspiration. It is true he never really forgot the claims of technique and the difficulty of maintaining its efficiency : " Without unceasing practice," he writes, " nothing can be done. Practice is Art. If you leave off, you are lost ; " and if on the whole he says little on this side of the matter, the reason no doubt is that he did much. Mrs. Blake assured a friend that she never saw her husband's hands idle. This fact, however, though it ensured his position as an artist, did nothing to correct the extravagant concentration of his theory, or to prevent it from re-acting in a very damaging manner upon his work. His theory, as he usually states it, leaves no room for the recognition of degrees in inspiration or in the artist's power to realise it. Either a work is inspired or it is not; if it is not inspired, it is not art; if it is, it is the gift of God, the ultimate true and beautiful is expressed in it, human power can go no further. This idea enables him without sacrifice of modesty, neither flinching nor discriminating, to place his own work on a level with that of the greatest names in history. " The artist," he writes in his *Descriptive Catalogue*, " knows that what he does is not inferior to the grandest Antiques. Superior it cannot be, for human power cannot go beyond either what he does or what they have done; it is the gift of God, it is inspiration and vision. . . . The human mind cannot go beyond the gift of God, the Holy Ghost. To suppose that Art can go beyond the finest specimens of Art that are now in the world is not knowing what Art is; it is being blind to the gifts of the Spirit." Passing our mind's eye over some of Blake's less fortunate adventures, we shall be inclined to feel that this is, so to speak, a little severe upon the Spirit. But he sometimes puts the point less paradoxically. Under Wordsworth's verses *To H. C.*, *six years old*, he wrote: " This is all in the highest degree imaginative, and equal to any poet, but not superior. I cannot think that real poets have any competition. None are greatest in the kingdom of heaven. It is so in poetry." Perhaps the reply to this may be that no real poet ever lived, and that art is an unrealised ideal ; still Blake's view recommends itself to a considerable body of critics, who hold that it is no part of true criticism to arrange artists or their works according to any order of merit ; but merely to decide whether they have achieved artistic expression, and, if so, to accept what they have done as final. However we may state the matter, what we cannot deny is that a great deal of work passed from Blake's hand as inspired, which cannot appear so to any but its producer. The most conspicuous, one might say the most flagrant, example of the illusion is to be found in the later Prophetic Books : these, according to Blake's account, were not composed by him, but dictated to him. They were inspired : and the inspiration spontaneously clothed itself in appropriate forms. "When this Verse was first dictated to me," he says, "I considered a monotonous cadence like that used by Milton and Shakespeare and all writers of English blank verse, derived from the modern bondage of rhyming,[1] to be a

---

[1] This statement must be noted as characteristic of Blake's habitual attitude to historic truth.

necessary and indispensable part of ‚verse. But I soon found that in the mouth of a true orator such monotony was not only awkward, but as much a bondage as rhyme itself. I therefore have produced a variety in every line, both of cadences and number of syllables. Every word and every letter is studied and put into its fit place; the terrific numbers are reserved for the terrific parts, the mild and gentle for the mild and gentle parts, and the prosaic for inferior parts; all are necessary to each other." Self-deception exudes from every pore of this piece of ingenuous yet laboured braggadocio. No one need be at pains to refer to the work it prefaces to see the absurdity of it; for it is manifestly inconsistent within itself. Wishing to insist on the imaginative or spontaneous quality of the work, Blake claims that it was dictated to him (mentioning elsewhere that he wrote it twenty or thirty lines at a time, and sometimes even against his will); wishing to reiterate his pet theory of " minute discrimination" he asserts that he " has produced a variety," and that " every word and every letter is studied." Which, one wonders, was the truth? Both cannot be. The idea of a marriage between inspiration and execution totters.

There is no doubt that Blake was stimulated to an excess of perversity by his revolt against the rationalistic theories to which Reynolds was at this time giving currency in his famous Presidential Addresses. Blake really has a high respect for Sir Joshua's opinion and is ready to quote it triumphantly when it agrees with his own. But he had an interview with Reynolds in early life, in which Reynolds advised him to correct his drawing. Blake drew under inspiration, and it was, therefore, to his mind, impossible that he should draw incorrectly. Reynolds was a blasphemer; Blake became, in the spiritual world, his life-long antagonist. Regarding Reynolds as the sworn enemy of enthusiasm, he thinks no execration too violent for him, no device or craft too low to be used as weapons for his spiritual discomfiture. He aptly describes in *Jerusalem* the temper which he uses in his attack. " Still I labour in hope," he writes, " though still my tears flow down, that he who will not defend Truth may be compelled to defend a Lie, that he may be snared and caught, that Enthusiasm and Life may not cease." Inspiration was naturally the main theme of their differences. With Blake, inspiration had, as we have seen, become a fetish. He was hopelessly at the mercy of everything that introduced itself to him under that title. This should be remembered whenever his comments on the Addresses are read. Every imaginative reader who can allow—as who has not now learned to allow ?—for

Blake's idiosyncrasies of manner, will tend to sympathise with the point of view he takes up. But
inspiration makes a dangerous *vade mecum*, and this is
a fact which Blake had never enough mental agility to
perceive. " What has reasoning to do with the art of
painting ? " he cries out against Reynolds, whose position as Presidential lecturer he seems to interpret as
a call to Prophecy ; and when Reynolds warns the
students against enthusiasms, and suggests that divine
inspiration and traffic with heaven for ideas are things
which they may be content to leave alone, Blake bursts
forth again : " And such is the coldness with which
Reynolds speaks, and such is his enmity ! Enthusiastic
admiration is the first principle of knowledge, and its
last. . . . The man who on examining his own mind
finds nothing of inspiration ought not to dare to be an
artist ; he is a fool, and a cunning knave, suited to the
purposes of evil demons. The man who never in his
mind and thought travelled to heaven is no artist."
Truth is with Blake certainly, but wisdom surely is
with Reynolds. The " poetic genius," as Blake himself
would have contended, is unteachable ; you either
have it, or not ; but Reynolds is speaking as a
teacher ; and if it is, on the one side, a weakness in
him to leave it too much out of count, the very
fact that no instruction can produce it, turns that

weakness into a kind of strength. Blake's antagonism is schoolboyish and immature. Just because it is the gift of God, inspiration does not need to be defended, and does not admit of being inculcated, by man.

Inspiration being the first topic on which Reynolds exposed himself to Blake's contempt and ridicule, the second was "General Ideas." Neither Reynolds nor Blake expresses himself with very great clearness on this topic, which, in fact, involves a problem of high complexity and interest. Reynolds incorporated in his lectures the rather vague language about it prevailing in his day. Blake replied with dogmatic denials which are probably to be considered the outcome of his experience as an engraver. Their duel begins in the introductory note to the Discourses, when the Editor speaks of Reynolds as a great generaliser and says that "generalising and classification is the great glory of the human mind." *Blake*: "To generalise is to be an Idiot. To particularise is the Alone Distinction of Merit." The central point at issue comes very early to the fore. In his first Discourse Reynolds narrates how Raphael "on the sight of the Capella Sistina, immediately from a dry Gothic and even insipid manner. which attends to the minute accidental discriminations of particular and individual objects, assumed that grand style of painting which improves partial representation by the general and invariable ideas of Nature." *Blake*: "Minute discrimination is not accidental. All sublimity is founded on minute discrimination." Again in the second Discourse: "Instead of copying the touches of those great masters, copy only their conceptions . . . Labour to invent on their general principles." *Blake*: "General principles again! Unless you consult particulars you cannot even know or see Michael Angelo or Raphael or anything else." *Reynolds*: "Though the painter is to overlook the accidental discriminations of nature, he is to exhibit distinctly, and with precision, the general forms of things." *Blake*: "Here he is for determinate, and yet for indeterminate. Distinct general form cannot exist. Distinction is particular, not general." *Reynolds*: "A firm and determined outline is one of the characteristics of the great style in painting, and, let me add, that he who possesses the knowledge of the exact form which every part of nature ought to have, will be fond of expressing that knowledge with correctness and precision in all his works." *Blake*: "A noble sentence. Here is a sentence which overthrows all his Book." It must be conceded that the remarks of Reynolds on this subject, though nearer truth than his remarks on enthusiasm and inspiration, are set in a context which

considerably impairs their value. Nor are they wise.
The attempt to provide a method on which students
may rise to a practice of the grand style in art is
singularly ill-judged. If it was a true instinct which led
Reynolds to leave genius out of his recommendations,
by the same instinct he should have spared any attempt
to formulate principles which genius alone can vivify.
Yet his main point is clear enough. An examination
of the noblest works of art reveals the fact that few of
the forms that appear in them are modelled precisely
after the pattern of any individual example—even a
representative example—such as might occur in a
natural context. You cannot match tree with tree, or
man with man. Even portraiture when great is always
imaginative and constructive. The artist has subjected the whole of his material to an operation which
modifies every component form. According to Reynolds, he has " generalised " it. Reynolds particularly
connects this operation with the branch of the art
called " history," by which he really meant monumental
figure design. The painter, he says, must disregard all
those qualities in his material that attach it to a particular time and place, and give it only those which it
might have in common with every example of its kind
—which might belong to it whatever place or time it
was attached to. He must say with Xeuxis—" in

aeternitatem pingo." Reynolds thus saw very clearly
what great art left out ; he did not see clearly enough
what it put in, and that its results were obtained not
by a process of rejection but by concentration, not by
sifting but by magnetism. In his seventh Discourse he
is guilty of a grave indiscretion : " We allow a poet,"
he says, " to express his meaning, when his meaning is
not well known to himself, with a certain degree of
obscurity, as it is one source of the sublime " : to which
Blake retorts conclusively that " Obscurity is neither
the source of the sublime nor of anything else." This
idea, that obscurity is an element from which sublimity
and grandeur proceed, is the idea which Blake detects
in all Reynolds's remarks on generalisation, and he is
right to protest against it. It springs up in Reynolds's
mind as the result of seeing the process on its negative
rather than on its positive side. Blake, who sees the
positive side only, dismisses everything that Reynolds
has to say for foolishness ; and his main contention
against Reynolds is a true one. All the component
parts of a work of art must, of course, to be right, be
particular to that work. A work of art, like everything else, is a combination of minute particulars.
Yet we must remember that when Reynolds says that
" A history painter paints man in general," he does not
deny this, and Blake's retort that " A history painter

paints the hero, and not man in general but most
minutely in particular " is a mere irrelevance ; and so
again where Reynolds says that " All smaller things,
however perfect in their way, are to be sacrificed without mercy to the greater," Blake's rejoinder " Sacrifice
the parts, what becomes of the whole ?." is folly. It
does not follow that the " greater things," because
greater, are to be expressed with less precision ; and
the only object of sacrificing the smaller things is to
keep them precise. For since in a work of art the number
of ideas that can be expressed is limited, there must be
a choice made ; and, if the main associations are to be
heroic, details that belong to the individual private
life will naturally prove irrelevant. To conceive the
hero we must, to adopt Reynolds's language, " generalise " ; to adopt Blake's language, we must construct a
whole of " minutely organised particulars " ; nothing
will be worth our attention in either case except what
contributes to the conception of heroism which it
is our aim to represent. The idea Reynolds wished
to formulate was indeed one on which Blake himself
insisted constantly : that great art studied what was
eternal ; and he recognised that this involved neglecting
the " minute accidental discriminations of particular
and individual objects." If, in replying, he had gone
no further than to say that " minute discrimination is

not accidental," no fault could have been found with
him. But he balances Reynolds's confusion of sublimity and vagueness with an equally serious confusion
of his own, and speaks as though the decisiveness of an
artist's purpose were to be judged by his power to
elaborate detail as detail. His own most fundamental
artistic gift, which was for the direct expression of the
emotions, demanded—and when he was working most
spontaneously could count on—a power of generalisation or of abstraction, to use a more appropriate term,
of the very subtlest and most elusive kind. Blake's
most successful figures are hardly figures at all ; rather
they are flames or waves of feeling which the human
form, as we know it, has been liquefied, rarified, to
express. The root of his contention is that the
creative mind knows instinctively what is relevant to
its purpose and what is not, and that the relevant is
always something definite and precise. Looking at the
matter more deeply, we see without a doubt that, in his
conception of what an artist has to do or does, he is
far more right than Reynolds. His remarks have the
incisiveness which comes of a direct application of
concrete experience. He works from the centre to the
circumference, striking out clear beams of intuition.
But his beams travel all one way : they do not radiate
at even distances : his wheel will not revolve. General-

isation, as Reynolds describes it, has, it is true enough, nothing to do with the production of a work of art; and even if we relate his description to the product rather than to the process, we shall still find it fumbling and faulty. But Blake, being pledged to uphold " vision " as " organised more minutely than anything in this vegetative world," redeemed his pledge by a display of irrelevant minuteness in his work which makes, and must continue to make, many even of his best designs the very abomination of desolation to an unbiassed intelligence. The minute organisation of ill-assorted muscles on a frame, which in its artistic setting has no more material significance than a film of vapour, proves nothing as to the accuracy of vision or the substantiality of its object. It merely proves that Blake by his theories and his antagonisms has destroyed the free growth of his artistic gift.

These theories are, as I said, probably traceable to his early training and constant practice as an engraver. This comes out clearly in the public address printed in Gilchrist's second volume and described as " intended to accompany Blake's engraving of the *Canterbury Pilgrims*." The main object of the address is to defend the clear dry style of engraving which Blake had learned from Basire, and Blake himself as its representative, against the softer Italian style which had just

come into vogue, and of which men like Schiavonetti
and Bartolozzi were exponents.   It is not necessary to
enter here into the question of the relative importance
of the two schools : to Blake's mind there never could
have been a question. That to which his own hand had
been formed, and to which as a consequence his visions
automatically accommodated themselves, could never to
him have appeared anything but the right one.   Thus
the theme may be conveniently treated in combination
with another main principle of his theory, that " Execution is the result of invention," or more poetically,
" the chariot of genius."   His views on this subject
were crystallised and intensified by Cromek's action in
choosing Schiavonetti as engraver of the designs to
Blair's *Grave*.   All Blake says about it, and he says
much that is bitter, is only to be understood in connection with the sense of disappointment and personal
affront which grew in his mind as the result of this
transaction.   Whether or not Cromek did him a good
turn in employing Schiavonetti is a question which
criticism does best to leave unanswered. The designs to
The Grave became the best known of his works. Schiavonetti's engraving was in the popular style.   But that
Schiavonetti instinctively " corrected " Blake, and that
in consequence some of the character and individuality
of Blake's conception was conventionalised and lost, is

a fact which, without help from Blake's heartrending lamentations, every keen observer will at once notice for himself. If Blake had had the commission, would this individuality have been carried to the pitch of monstrous exaggeration which makes the designs to Young's *Night Thoughts* so vacuous and so distasteful, or would he have worked after the manner which makes his engraving of the *Canterbury Pilgrims* so peculiar and yet so great? In depriving posterity of the second, Schiavonetti saved it from the first. Yet there is a certain conventionalisation of insipidity in the opening design, which, just because it almost makes insipidity pass muster, is perhaps a worse offence than any Blake himself could have committed. And this conventionalisation, this softening, with "all the beauties paled out, blurred and blotted," is what Blake's paternal eye discovered in every fragment of Schiavonetti's translation of his work. Blake's injury was so acute that only epigram could give him relief. His spleen vented itself in spasms of high-flavoured satirical invective, and in the public address just mentioned he has some eloquent sentences elaborating the same ideas. "No man can improve on original invention, nor can an original invention exist without execution organised, delineated, and articulated either by God or man: I do not mean smoothed up and niggled and pocopen'd . . . but drawn with a firm and decided hand at once, like Michael Angelo, Shakespeare, and Milton." Blake's training had led him to conceive this clearness and decisiveness of intention as a quality peculiar to the draughtsman: "Painting is drawing on canvas, and engraving is drawing on copper, and nothing else;" and by drawing he meant line-work. "I do not pretend to engrave finer than Albert Durer:" (!) "but I do pretend to engrave finer than Strange, Woollett, Hall, or Bartolozzi; and all because I understand drawing, which they understood not. Englishmen have been so used to journeyman's bungling that they cannot bear the firmness of a master's touch. Every line is the line of beauty: it is only fumble and bungle that cannot draw a line." Thus the term "drawing" came to be used by him as a sort of mystic symbol to represent any kind of work, whether in painting or in poetry, which showed the quality of organised conception, the only quality he valued; and he was led by this to heap contempt on all the works of the great colourists, simply because he could not see what they were at. "The unorganised blots and blurs of Rubens and Titian are not art, nor can their method ever express ideas or imaginations, any more than Pope's metaphysical jargon of rhyming. Unappropriate execution is the most nauseous of all

affectation and foppery." And here in the very heat
of his denunciations he seems almost to stumble upon
the truth. What if the despised Rubens and Titian
had ideas of their own, to which their blotting, blur-
ring method was after all appropriate? If Blake could
have seen so much as the possibility of this he must
have been a new man ; his theory demanded the recognition of it at least as a possibility ; and so much he
actually admits, but brushes the whole matter aside in
a splendid passion of paradox. His first principle
being that invention dictates its appropriate execution,
his second that varieties of execution are all varieties of
drawing, he proceeds : " I do not condemn Rubens,
Rembrandt, and Titian because they did not understand drawing, but because they did not understand
colouring ; how long shall I be forced to beat this into
men's ears ? I do not condemn Strange or Woollett
because they did not understand drawing, but because
they did not understand engraving. I do not condemn
Pope or Dryden because they did not understand
imagination, but because they did not understand
verse. Their colouring, graving and verse can never be
applied to art : that is not either colouring, graving,
or verse, which is unappropriate to the subject." But
what was really wrong with all of them in Blake's eyes
was that he looked in vain in their works for the wiry

I

line of articulate invention; everything that could not
be classed as drawing was, to his mind, *ipso facto*, in-
appropriate: "Moderns," he elsewhere says, "wish to
draw figures without lines, and with great and heavy
shadows; are not shadows more unmeaning than lines,
and more heavy? Oh! who can doubt this?" And
finally in a passage in which all the mystic presupposi-
tions are brought out, and which must be regarded as
the *locus classicus* upon the subject—" The distinction
that is made in modern times between a painting and
a drawing proceeds from ignorance of art. The merit
of a picture is the same as the merit of a drawing.
The dauber daubs his drawings; he who draws his
drawings draws his pictures. . . . The great and golden
rule of art, as well as of life, is this: that the more
distinct, sharp and wiry the bounding line, the more
perfect the work of art; and the less keen and sharp
the greater is the evidence of weak imitation, plagiarism
and bungling. . . . How do we distinguish one face or
countenance from another, but by the bounding line
and its infinite inflexions and movements? What is it
that builds a house and plants a garden, but the
definite and determinate? What is it that distin-
guishes honesty and knavery, but the hard and wiry
line of rectitude and certainty in the actions and
intentions? Leave out the line, and you leave out life

itself; all is chaos again, and the line of the Almighty must be drawn out upon it before man or beast can exist. Talk no more then of Correggio or Rembrandt, or any other of the plagiaries of Venice or Flanders." All this, as I said, while on the one hand it very forcibly expresses a truth which like most truths is self-evident when you see it,—namely, that every part, every least part of a work of art is meaningless, unless it has a meaning ; and that, however you choose to define this meaning, whether as character, tone, expression, or what not, it arises from an infinitesimal precision and exactitude in the handling of the material that conveys it, by which it is constituted just itself and nothing else—on the other hand exemplifies that very fallacy of generalisation against which we saw Blake earlier fulminating. To generalise, when generalisation takes such forms as this, is to be an idiot indeed. Because Blake thought in line, because line was the medium in which his gospel of exactitude was revealed to him, he supposed it the only medium which admitted such exactitude. When he says there is no way to distinguish one face from another but by the bounding line, the crudity of his prejudice becomes startlingly clear.

Blake's contempt for the works of the great colourists did not prevent him from forming elaborate theories as to what the ideal in colouring should be. It would

appear that so far as this branch of the art was concerned he was completely self-taught: this made him
if anything more, rather than less, dogmatic about it;
and not unnaturally it was in this branch that he was
able to announce a splendid invention to the world!
His ideas on the subject can be approached best
through a consideration of his leading prejudice. At
that period of his life at which we first come intimately
into touch with him through the letters and printed
catalogues, we find him entering upon and establishing
himself in an unconquerable aversion to the use of oils.
In the fifth letter published by Mr. A. G. B. Russell,
and dated 1799, Blake writes to Dr. Trusler: " If you
approve of my manner, and it is agreeable to you, I
would rather paint pictures in oil of the same dimensions than make drawings, and on the same terms ";
and it seems fairly conjecturable from this that oil was
a medium in which he had at least experimented. But
the " species of tempera " referred to by Mr. Russell in
a note, which Blake invented as more suitable to his
purpose, was so peculiar a species that it has become
a grave question among connoisseurs whether any of
Blake's pictures are worked in oils at all. The works
described by Mr. Russell on pages xxvi and xxvii of
his Introduction were all exhibited at the Carfax
Gallery in 1906, and, in the admirable catalogue pre-

pared by Messrs. Adey and Ross, were without exception pronounced executed in tempera. It is not even certain that oil was used for the colour-prints, for which it might naturally have been supposed to be an appropriate medium. In reconstructing Blake's artistic history upon the basis of statements made in his letters Mr. Russell is straying upon dangerous ground. It is clear that Blake believed himself, both before and after his journey to Felpham, to be passing through a time of doubt and affliction in the things relating to the spirit, that is, to his art. But exactly what this affliction may have amounted to, translated into the terms of everyday life and speech, is a much more difficult matter to decide. Blake may have had the intention at one time "to incorporate into his work all the graces of Venice and Flanders as well as the linear austerity of the Florentines," but my impression would be that his existing works offer a meagre basis for the discovery of any clear evidence of such intention, and that it is better to regard it as having remained purely internal. In the same way his outburst of joy on visiting the Truchsessian Gallery in 1804 cannot really, I think, be associated with any observable change in his methods either of execution or of design. And so in regard to the letter to Dr. Trusler : it is a reply, and we do not know what Dr. Trusler had said to Blake by way of provocation. Possibly he had suggested that Blake was incapable of painting in oils; perhaps the names of Teniers and Rembrandt were mentioned by Dr. Trusler as likely to be unfamiliar to him. If so, Blake's rejoinder that he had studied Rembrandt and Teniers no less than Raphael and Michael Angelo need not be taken very seriously. Blake could say the most astounding things when he was put to it. If we turn to a letter to Mr. Butts, dated three years later, we shall find the following: " I have now given two years to the intense study of those parts of the art which relate to light and shade and colour, and am convinced that either my understanding is incapable of comprehending the beauties of colouring, or the pictures which I painted for you are equal in every part of the art, and superior in one, to anything that has been done since the age of Raphael. All Sir J. Reynolds's discourses to the Royal Academy will show that the Venetian finesse in art can never be united with the majesty of colouring necessary to historical beauty." The intense study Blake alludes to is very likely to be associated with the three pictures called experiment pictures in the *Descriptive Catalogue*, " painted at intervals for experiment on colours " but again " without any oily vehicle." " Clear colours, unmuddied by oil " are his ideal: and he goes on, " Oil has falsely been supposed to give strength to colours, but a little consideration must show the fallacy of this opinion." "Frescoes," on the other hand, "are as high finished as miniatures or enamels, and they are known to be unchangeable." It should be remembered that the period was one in which connoisseurship had no eye for anything but "tone," and had a very limited conception even of what tone might be. Sir George Beaumont's assertion that the colour of a good picture should match that of an old violin represented a point of view which a painter so different from Blake as Constable had to spend the best part of his life protesting against. Thus Blake's prejudice against oils must be connected, partly of course, with the fact that he did not understand the use of them, but principally with the natural revulsion inspired in him by the prevailing worship of monotony and dinginess, for which he made the use of oils responsible, as also with his horror of those "idiot's arts" of blending, to which work in oils so admirably lends itself.

What then of Blake's Frescoes? The reader will most quickly recognise the temper of mind in which Blake approached such a matter by hearing him speak for himself. In addition to his now famous *Descriptive Catalogue*, Blake issued a single-page leaflet in advertisement of his exhibition, and, this not being printed in Gilchrist's *Life*, it may be of interest to quote the more important section of the text in full. The front is occupied by a description of the chief exhibits and closes with the quotation " Fit audience find tho' few. Milton." The reverse side is headed " The Invention of a Portable Fresco," and runs as follows :

A wall on canvas or wood or any other portable thing of dimensions ever so large or ever so small, which may be removed with the same convenience as so many easel pictures, is worthy the consideration of the rich and those who have the direction of Public works.   If the Frescoes of Appelles, of Protogenes, of Raphael, or Michael Angelo, could have been removed, we might perhaps have them now in England.   I could divide Westminster Hall or the Walls of any other great building into compartments and ornament them with Frescoes which would be removable at pleasure.

Oil will not drink or absorb colour enough to stand the test of very little Time, and of the Air: it grows yellow and at length brown.   It was never generally used till after Vandyke's time.   All the little old pictures, called Cabinet pictures, are in Fresco and not in Oil.   Fresco painting is properly Miniature or Enamel painting ; everything in Fresco is as high finished as Miniature or Enamel, although in works larger than life.   The Art has been lost ; I have recovered it.   How this was done will be told together with the whole Process by a work on Art now in the Press.   The ignorant insults of individuals will not hinder me from doing my duty to my Art.   Fresco

Painting as it is now practised is like most other things, the contrary of what it pretends to be. The execution of my designs being all in Water Colours (that is in Fresco) was regularly refused to be exhibited by the R.A. and the British Institution has this year followed its example and has effectually excluded me by this Resolution. I therefore invite those Noblemen and Gentlemen who are its Subscribers to inspect what they have excluded, and those who have been told that my works are but an unscientific and irregular Eccentricity, a Madman's Scrawls, I demand of them to do me the justice to examine before they decide.

There cannot be more than two or three great Painters or Poets in any Age or Country, and these in a corrupt state of Society are easily excluded but not so easily obstructed. They have excluded Water Colours : it is therefore become necessary that I should exhibit to the Public in an exhibition of my own my Designs, painted in Water Colours. If Italy is enriched and made great by Raphael, if Michael Angelo is its supreme glory, if Art is the glory of a Nation, if Genius and Inspiration are the great Origin and Bond of Society, the distinction my Works have gained from those who best understand such things calls for my Exhibition as the greatest of Duties to my country.

WILLIAM BLAKE.

The interest of this effusion is, of course, mainly psychological. My purpose in printing it was to show that serious criticism of this part of Blake's theorising is quite beside the mark. As a matter of fact the number of works by Blake in which colour is the essential medium of expression are comparatively few: he had an intense delight in freshness and radiancy of tint and an exquisite sense for harmonies in radiance: Gilchrist's praise of a coloured copy of the *America*, that, as you turn the leaves, "it is sometimes like an increase of daylight upon the retina," suggests the height of Blake's achievement in this branch of the art: but his use of colour is in the main symbolical and decorative, and rather accompanies than expresses the form: he is more an illuminator than a painter. As to his rediscovery of the art of fresco, by which he intended not fresco but tempera, and which, portable, or permanent, was no discovery—for the method he hit on, though different from any that had been used by the old tempera painters, has not justified the claims he made for it—as for the materials he worked with, the ground on which his paint was laid, or his peculiar tastes in varnish, gum and glue, all these things are of interest to the craftsman who can profit by the errors as well as by the success of a predecessor, and to the connoisseur for whom the artist's eccentricities are valuable as giving an extra rarity to his work. Here it hardly concerns us to do more than to repeat that it was Blake's ignorance in this department that gave him

TITLE-PAGE TO "AMERICA"
BRITISH MUSEUM

To face p. 138

such limitless scope for originality; his self-assurance, that left him in no doubt that the forgotten secrets of the old masters were in his hand (his work on art theories and methods never saw the light); while, for all that, his genius enabled him now and again to use his materials, whether wood, canvas, or copper, whether drawing, or painting, or printing, with exquisite appropriateness and supreme effect.

Blake was so independent a spirit and so ignorant a man, that he occupies, and would have wished to occupy, no definable position in the history of artistic tendencies and schools. He was at once too prejudiced and too profound. His prejudices were in part the outcome of his apprenticeship to Basire and the long course of study in Gothic forms which was incidental to that apprenticeship. The latter was among the most lasting influences in his art, and, in suggesting that it was harmful, I should not mean to deny that Blake's deepest affinities were with the Gothic mood. But the best Gothic has a certain chastening humility about it which Blake lacked. It is individualistic, but its individualism has a corporate basis. Blake's was a defiant individualism, and the association of this with an early acquaintance with the eccentricities of Gothic form was one of the sources of nightmare in his work. It also thus comes about that in praising Raphael and

Michael Angelo he praises them rather for what they share with all great artists than for any qualities peculiar to them. They are mystic names to him, types of the consummate in art; they occupy a cloud region in his mind side by side with the " lost art of the Greeks," or with " the greater works of the Asiatic Patriarchs," which " with their accompaniments were terrific and grand in the highest degree." His unconscious assimilation of their style was harmful to him; he got insipidity from Raphael and muscles from Michael Angelo. He recognises the spirit which governed them, enters into it, shares it; but it becomes in him the spirit of vain-glory, because it pretends to work without an instrument. All Blake's art-criticism must be read, like almost everything else he wrote, in a symbolical sense. If he makes a statement of fact, it is prudent to take for granted that he is wrong. To enter into a discussion of his criticisms of Rembrandt, Titian, Correggio, would be to misunderstand their import. Those names, as used by him, have little or nothing to do with the historic figures which civilisation associates with them. They are symbols of certain incidental impressions made upon Blake's mind, the names attached to them being those of the men from whom he thought they were derived. His Rembrandt is neither more nor less like ours than his Jerusalem like our Jerusalem. None of these criticisms or enthusiasms, therefore, can rightly come up for discussion here.

So far we have dealt only with Blake's ideas about Art in the common acceptance of the term: to get a completer view of his theory we have still to consider it in a wider context, and attempt to see Art, not as one among a number of human activities, but as Blake himself saw it, that is, as the essential activity of man, the ideal type to which all man's action must conform itself—human life in epitome. With this aim, we may glance first at his conception of art in its relation to society; and second in its relation to religion. A difficulty connected with the first branch of the inquiry is that Blake's conception of society was of so elementary a kind as hardly to deserve the name of a conception: he had, therefore, no difficulty in relating his idea of art to it. There was hardly more to be done than to introduce into a vacant area of his mind ideas which had been formed already in the area dedicated to art: it was not a matter of mutual accommodation: it was merely an extension of the artistic principle to a fresh kind of subject-matter. Something of the confusion with which it was Blake's habit to express himself on

this kind of topic may be gleaned from the following sentences which, among a host of others, are
inscribed in festoons about an engraved copy of the
Laocoon : " Good and Evil are Riches and Poverty ; a
tree of misery, propagating generation and death."
" Hebrew Art is called Sin by the Deist Science."
" Where any view of Money exists, Art cannot be carried
on, but War only, by pretences to the two impossibilities, Chastity and Abstinence, Gods of the Heathen."
" For every pleasure Money is useless." " The Old and
New Testaments are the great code of Art. Art is the
Tree of Life. Science is the Tree of Death. The whole
business of man is the Arts and All things in common.
No secrecy is Art." [1] These sentences, in their general
tenor, show that Blake identifies the artistic spirit
with that so well-known spirit in society which asserts
that the problems of life are produced by looking for
them, and that for those who see no problem, none
exists. He finds the distinction between wealth and
poverty as unreal as the distinction between good and
evil ; the pure mind does not recognise it ; it comes of

[1] Blake often speaks of science side by side with art, classing
them together as spiritual activities ; but here he is thinking of it
upon its negative side, and as usual makes in regard to the whole a
statement which he does not intend to apply to more than a part.
Seeing science thus he denounces it as the Tree of Death ; elsewhere
he calls it Christianity.

eating of the fruit of the forbidden tree. Perhaps he means no more than that the true pleasures are those that money cannot buy; that it is of the very essence of the spiritual delight that it should be shareable, and that to understand is to desire to share it. "No secrecy is Art."

> Since all the riches of this world
>   May be gifts from the devil and earthly kings,
> I should suspect that I worshipped the devil
>   If I thanked my God for worldly things.
>
> The countless gold of a merry heart,
>   The rubies and pearls of a loving eye,
> The idle man never can bring to the mart,
>   Nor the cunning hoard up in his treasury.

A few more sentences from other sources complete the outline of Blake's idea of art in this relation. His natural predilection for agricultural and pastoral metaphor makes many of his expressions a singular anticipation of the maturer utterances of Ruskin. Ruskin's "Soldiers of the Ploughshare instead of Soldiers of the Sword" is prettily forestalled by a couplet in *Auguries of Innocence*,

> When gold and gems adorn the plough
> To peaceful arts shall envy bow.

and with a more poetical elusiveness in the following quatrain :

> The sword sang on the barren heath,
>   The sickle in the fruitful field ;
> The sword he sang a song of death
>   But could not make the sickle yield.

Whenever Blake's wildness or extravagance of expression offends us we must remember that he was a perverted lyrist. If only the horrid symbolic systematising had not got hold of him, we should have been able to accept all his main utterances as profoundly and often exquisitely expressing, not indeed truth realised as a system, but the whole trend and current of those spiritual energies which spring from righteousness and have truth for their goal. The *Auguries of Innocence*, a poem as perfect as any that he wrote, gives us a key to an understanding of all his aphoristic paradoxes; its opening couplet

> A Robin Redbreast in a cage
> Puts all heaven in a rage

may be compared with the more complex assertion that " Poetry fettered fetters the human race." In Blake's eyes these sayings are an expression of one truth ; but the second, just because it is in prose, is the more dangerous, and leads us to see how its author came to view all method and education as a fetter to the spirit, to think of men as robins, and of society as an institution framed for caging them.

Where Blake touches the relation of art to religion he seems at first sight even more paradoxical, but is in fact much less so. Society does not pretend to be more than a mechanism, providing ways and means; and if everything that is mechanical is confining, society is undoubtedly a cage : related to human aspiration it is at best a ladder, and Blake will have nothing but wings. Just because religion is nearer to the centre and the heart of things, there is more reason in applying to it this ultimate standard of spontaneity. Where religion is concerned Blake will have nothing but the spirit : " *The whole* of the New Church," he writes, " is in the active life and not in ceremonies at all," and in this, and we may at once say in all else, he thinks and speaks of art and religion as identified. It ought not to be forgotten—it is I think too often forgotten—that Blake's greatness cannot be separated from his creed. He has penetrated with unerring insight to the essence and principle of Christianity, and applies it with never-wavering conviction to the very department of man's activity, which to many minds appears most nearly allied to Paganism. There are few things more

K

interesting to note than the enthusiasm with which
Blake's work has been taken up in recent years by a
school of critics to whom art presents itself primarily
as a study in sensuous impressions, and for whom therefore his identification of art with Christianity remains
wholly meaningless.   When he compares love in conduct with imagination in art, and demands complete
freedom for both, he wins the applause of many, who
suppose the ideal life he recommends to be that of a kind
of careless Bacchus, who redeems his amatory inclina-
tions by making them a theme for verse.   But when he
asserts that " Jesus and his Apostles and Disciples were
all artists " and that " A poet, a painter, a musician, an
architect, the man or woman who is not one of these is
not a Christian,"[1] they begin to suspect that he is
breaking into the charmed circle with an irrelevant
idea.   Yet this apparent irrelevance is to Blake the
very core of truth.   When Dr. Trusler disapproves of
his designs, he sees at once that their differences are at
root religious.   " I could not help smiling," he writes
to Cumberland, " at the difference between the doc-
trines of Dr. Trusler and those of Christ."   Dr. Trusler,
however, stood for the " idiot reason " and the dif-

---

[1] Of course meaning that the true religious life takes form in
action flowing, as all true artistic creation flows, spontaneously from
the heart : that is, under the inspiration of the divine Love.

THE HYMN OF CHRIST AND THE APOSTLES
W. GRAHAM ROBERTSON, ESQ.

To face p. 146

ference Blake would now smile at, if he found matter
in it for smiling, would be on the other side of the
fence. Gilchrist maintains that his identification of
Art with Christianity meant no more than that the
idea pleased him and that in consequence "his heart
told him that it was true." Very few of Blake's ideas
have, in fact, any other sanction. He thought what
it pleased him to think. But his idea of Christianity
as Art is one of the most fundamental and one of the
most explicit of his ideas. And there is none that
rouses him to a greater passion of feeling. Indeed we
are touching here not upon his theory but upon himself. Art was his one activity, and with him it was a
religious activity in the fullest sense of the word : " *The
whole* of the New Church is in the active life." He could
not in himself distinguish his religion from his art: " I
know of no other Christianity, and of no other Gospel,
than the liberty both of body and mind to exercise the
divine Arts of Imagination." Perhaps it is his highest
and noblest achievement to have maintained in his life
a genuine fusion of the two.

CHAPTER VIII

SYMBOLISM IN POETRY AND ART.
THE PROPHETIC BOOKS

REGARDING Blake as far as possible from the point of view of general culture, one of the principal questions we need to consider is that of the place of symbolism in art and in life. The pursuit of this theme cannot fail to involve us in problems of extreme complexity, and we shall do well to come to a preliminary understanding with our readers as to what a symbol is. A symbol, then, is a sign : the letter O symbolises a certain sound producible by my organs of speech ; when I see the letter, I think of the sound, and perhaps produce, or imagine myself producing it. Any other shape would have answered the purpose almost as well. But, as a matter of fact, this shape has a peculiar appropriateness because, as I produce the sound, my lips have a tendency to form themselves to a circle, and the one circle naturally leads the mind on to the other. A symbol, however, to be serviceable, must be something more than a mere sign.

Symbols become serviceable so far as they are *accepted* as signs of agreement, " treaties " between different minds; and the value of a system of symbols— such as the alphabet or the algebraical signs, or the code used in telegraphy—varies according to the number of people who consent to use it. Clearly it is a matter of immense convenience to the English, French, and allied races, that they share the same alphabetical signs; and further advantages would accrue if a common language could be decided on. But there is another side to the question. Every symbol implies the existence of a thing symbolised, and the extension in the use of the symbol cannot fruitfully proceed into countries where men are unfamiliar with the signified thing, and unable to form a clear conception of its nature. Now, in language, the most important symbols, or words, must always be those which give their names to the facts of human life itself, particularly to the inner life of the thoughts and the emotions. This inner life is made up of a complex of elements, playing most delicately one upon another, and, however deeply we may be convinced as to a fundamental unity of principle, we all admit that in different nations the complex is differently adjusted, and that the common humanity is expressed in different forms. Suppose, therefore, the existence of a common language, it follows that a number of the chief words composing it—among them all the words about which, ultimately, it is of the highest importance that no confusion shall arise—will carry various shades of meaning, according to the various nationality of the speakers ; they will be forced to use the same word for what to each of them will be a slightly different thing ; to one sign will correspond a variety of things signified ; and thus the initial compact and sustaining principle of the system will be violated, and the symbols, in proportion as they become more and more vague in reference, will lose their value. It seems clear that, from the beginning, a symbolic system is to be regarded merely as a means, to be appraised according to its degree of efficiency in securing a particular end in view. The mind only makes progress while it remains in living touch with the results of its previous activities ; and the extent to which this is possible depends on the conciseness of symbolic system in which these results are tabulated. Now nothing is more deadening, nothing hampers more the activity of the mind, than to be called upon to memorise meaninglessly. The inventor of a useless set of symbols —just so far as he succeeds in inflicting the burden of them upon others—must be regarded, from the point of view of culture, as a sort of criminal in disguise.

How then is symbolism to be regarded as it enters into the constitution of a work of art ? I would reply with the

assertion that the principles underlying art and symbolism are directly antagonistic.   The artist is no
system-maker.   It is not his aim to invent tags or labels
to be attached to known impressions, and so re-summon
them to the mind.   His aim is rather to detach himself
from those in use already, so as more freely to approach
the reality that underlies them, and to create a new and
living impression of it.   The antagonism is complete.
Yet we must note that the artist, because the material
he works with is limited in its scope, constantly relies
upon symbols as a means to stimulate the mind and
enable it to concentrate upon the particular aspect of
reality which he wishes to reveal, using them as a
shorthand code for matters which are subsidiary and
inessential; or it may even be, as in the case of the
poet, that an accepted symbolic system may itself form
the material with which he works.   On the other hand,
if we except symbolic codes scientifically adapted to a
highly abstract purpose, it will appear that the maintenance of a symbolic system seems to require the
presence in it of essentially artistic elements; the
symbols of which it is composed must not be mere
symbols; there must, as in the case of the letter O referred to earlier, be some kind of recognisable affinity
between the symbol and its signification.   And the
necessity for this increases with the complexity of the

system, or, in other words, according to the range of the realities to which it professes to provide an index.

It is this last consideration which occasions or explains the development of a more elaborate symbolism, a symbolism known as mystical, which, because it aims at providing the key to secret chambers of reality removed from the intercourse of everyday life, is often, in a confused way, regarded as, on that account, nearer to poetry; although, just so far as it perceives and follows a method of its own, that method must be the reverse of the poetical, must be fatal to the free growth of artistic expression. The assumption with which the mystic symbolist sets out is that there is a complete break between what is called on one side the natural or material world, and what on the other is called the spiritual. He believes that the spiritual world is that to which the human soul is native, but that the whole range of its normal observation and experience is confined to the world of nature. Explanations of a somewhat arbitrary kind are adduced to gloss over this state of exile— cosmogonies, psychologies of the Divine, and so forth. Blake himself spoke of the Creation as an "act of mercy." We need not concern ourselves with these, for they only arise as a result of the supposed intuition, by which the natural and spiritual are recognised as discrete. Man, it is asserted, being a spirit, has spiritual

faculties which place him in immediate touch with the
spiritual world ; but, living in the natural world, and
having developed natural faculties for the sustainment
of his life there, he is in danger of allowing his spiritual
faculties to rust from disuse. And now a curious fact
comes to his aid. For, in spite of the divorce between
the spiritual and the natural, the natural world is still
—it is never defined how—founded upon the spiritual,
and all its forms and all its processes have a counterpart
there. Thus, though the natural faculties observing
natural facts, perceive their natural qualities alone, these
same facts, observed by the spiritual faculties,[1] have
power to suggest the presence of a higher truth, of which
they are a shadow, and to direct the mind to contem-
plation, not of the natural world, in which it is an exile,
but of the spiritual, in which it is at home. In consequence, there is a system of thought developed, according
to which the value or importance of all natural phenomena depends upon the degree in which suggestions are
to be found in them of the spiritual realities to which
they point. And such a system is described as a symbolic system, because the natural phenomena are regarded as valueless in themselves, significant only in so

---

[1] Of course if spiritual and natural really were discrete the assumption here made that the natural fact could come under spiritual
observation would be quite unverifiable.

far as they stand for something beyond them, in the same way that a word has no meaning except as attached to the object which it names.

Now, as we saw earlier, the value of a symbol is in proportion to the exactitude with which those who use it conceive the reality of which it is a sign. In proportion as this reality is conceived more vaguely, the value of the symbol declines, until, at a certain point of vagueness, the possibility of using symbols at all becomes dependent upon the extent to which metaphorical resemblances present themselves to make the symbol not merely a sign but a suggestion of the object. This element of suggestion is really an intrusive element, it is the intrusion of the imitative, the artistic principle. Every symbolic system will avail itself, wherever possible, of such intrusion, because it gives an instinctive pleasure and aids memory thereby. But system is the life of symbolism, and this imitative principle will not submit to system. There is no method, therefore, of building up symbolic suggestion into a system but by recourse to the unsatisfactory frame of mind in which everything appears comparable, indiscriminately, with everything else. The point will become clear in an illustration. In a chapter of the first volume of their *Life and Works of William Blake*, entitled "The Necessity of Symbolism," Messrs. Ellis and Yeats refer to Shakespeare's comparison of Lear's mind to the vexed sea, and observe that it at once tells us something

more laden with meaning than many pages of psychology. A "correspondence," for the very reason that it is implicit rather than explicit, says far more than a syllogism or a scientific observation. The chief difference between the metaphors of poetry and the symbols of mysticism is that the latter are woven together into a complete system. The "vexed sea" would not be merely a detached comparison, but, with the fish it contains, would be related to the land and air, the winds and shadowing clouds, and all in their totality compared to the mind in its totality.

Nothing could be more precisely to our purpose. The sea not being, to Shakespeare, a symbol of the mind, the fact that it is bounded by earth and air, and that the mind is not so bounded, does not hamper him in in the least when he sets about comparing them one with another. Imagine fish in the mad mind of Lear! The symbolist's method, as Messrs. Ellis and Yeats explain to us, is different, and it is far more cumbrous. Seizing first a point of analogy such as Shakespeare has here expressed, the symbolist makes that point of analogy the excuse for a complete identification. He proceeds to say "sea" when he means "mind." Sea now, for him, *is* mind : and as there are clouds over the

sea and fish in it, it follows, demonstrably, that there
must be clouds over and fish in the mind.   Once this is
decided, nothing, of course, can be simpler than to find
out what they are.   You have only to follow out the
principle on which you began, namely, that a point of
resemblance or analogy is sufficient to justify symbolic
identification, and mental clouds and mental fishes will
multiply under your hands like microbes ; and you will
soon find yourself able to write a history of King Lear
without once mentioning the hero's name, picturing at
last his frenzy and death as the capture and defeat of a
sperm-whale by a cuttle-fish! It would be poor
practice to make sport of this method, if it were not for
the degree of nonsense of which its exponents themselves
make it a vehicle, and that this nonsense gains some
currency because associated with the name of poetry
and because flashes of true poetic insight are incorporated with it and are often to a considerable extent
conditioned by or incidental to it.   Blake's work teems
with such nonsense ; and, it should be added, the higher
the poetic insight of the mind by which this method is
adopted, the more dangerous because the more deceptive
is the nonsense in which it results.

Let us recur then to a consideration of the pure
poetic principle, of which this method is the counterfeit.
The systems of mystic symbolism are founded, as we

saw, on a metaphysical belief that nature is the pattern or shadow of a higher, spiritual reality, with which the mind of man may hold immediate communion. A similar conception underlies the impulse which finds expression in art and poetry. The mind, observing nature and itself as a part of nature, perceives everywhere, in the inexhaustible variety of natural objects and events and processes, a certain community of different things with one another and of all with itself: the quality of the whole appears in every part, and, though the parts as parts are finite, yet the perception in them of this organic relation to the whole gives to each an infinite significance. And the impulse to poetry may be described as the impulse to express that living vision to which the part appears not as a part merely, but with the light of the infinite upon it, and to show how the universal life is at work minutely and perfectly here too, and here, as everywhere, builds order and clothes itself in beauty. A conception somewhat of this kind underlies the poetic impulse and is the element which it shares with the impulse to symbolic mysticism. But poetry separates itself sharply from mysticism in the fact that it makes no effort to adopt a conscious methodical use of this conception. Symbolism takes its stand upon a theory clearly formulated, if intuitively perceived, that, in the last resort, everything

is like everything else : wielding this weapon, it can
conjure forth the sublimest of cloud castles, and violate
with impunity every principle of earthly architecture.
But the poet formulates no theory, because he is instinctively aware that no theory can embrace the fact : he
has no proud castle of metaphor to build up : he is
content to catch at such occasional resemblances as
actually present themselves to his mind ; and the nature
of these is to be fleeting.   If he sees the mind like the
vexed sea, he says so : if he sees it like a fish in the
vexed sea, he says that as well.   But the resemblance to
which he calls attention is for him the only interesting
point of connection between the two.   And the moment
he has expressed it he has done with it.   For the same
power which enables him to compare the mind and the
sea enables him also to distinguish between them, and
gives him the vision of ten thousand qualities in each,
which hold them eternally asunder.   To make the sea
a symbol of the mind is to lose the benefit of the ten
thousand qualities in which they differ, for the sake of
the few in which they agree.   And it is the death of
poetry.   For poetry is truth and freedom.

A typical passage taken from the less unintelligible
strata of Blake's mystical writing may enable us to
exemplify and develop some of these principles.   The
following is from the most elaborate of his works, from

And the voices of Bath & Canterbury & York & Edinburgh Cry
Over the Plow of Nations in the strong hand of Albion thundering along
Among the Fires of the Druid & the deep black rethundering Waters
Of the Atlantic which poured in impetuous loud loud louder & louder.
And the Great Voice of the Atlantic howled over the Druid Altars:
Weeping over his Children in Stone-henge in Maldon & Colchester.
Round the Rocky Peak of Derbyshire London Stone & Rosamonds Bower

What is a Wife & what is a Harlot? What is a Church? & What
Is a Theatre? are they Two & not One? can they Exist Separate?
Are not Religion & Politics the Same Thing? Brotherhood is Religion
O Demonstrations of Reason Dividing Families in Cruelty & Pride!

But Albion fled from the Divine Vision with the Plow of Nations enflaming
The Living Creatures maddend and Albion fell into the Furrow, and
The Plow went over him & the Living was Plowed in among the Dead
But his Spectre rose over the starry Plow. Albion fled beneath the Plow
Till he came to the Rock of Ages, & he took his Seat upon the Rock.
Wonder seizd all in Eternity. to behold the Divine Vision. open
The Center into an Expanse, & the Center rolled out into an Expanse

FORMS OF CITIES
BRITISH MUSEUM

To face p. 159

the poem for which, introducing it to the reader, he claims that " every word and every letter is studied and put into its fit place. . . . All are necessary to each other."

And this is the Song of Los, the Song that he sings
    on his Watch.
O lovely mild Jerusalem! O Shiloh of Mount
    Ephraim!
I see thy Gates of precious stones; thy Walls of gold
    and silver.
Thou art the soft reflected Image of the Sleeping Man
Who, stretched on Albion's rocks, reposes amidst his
    twenty-eight
Cities: where Beulah lovely terminates in the hills
    and valleys of Albion.
Cities not yet embodied in Time and Space: plant ye
The Seeds, O sisters, in the bosom of Time and Space's
    womb
To spring up for Jerusalem: lovely shadow of sleep-
    ing Albion,
Why wilt thou rend thyself apart and build an Earthly
    Kingdom
To reign in pride and to oppress and to mix the Cup
    of Delusion.
O thou that dwellest with Babylon! Come forth,
    O lovely one,
I see thy form, O lovely mild Jerusalem, wing'd with
    Six Wings,

In the opacous Bosom of the Sleeper, lovely three
    fold,
In Head and Heart and Reins, three Universes of
    love and beauty.
Thy forehead bright, Holiness to the Lord, with
    Gates of pearl
Reflects eternity beneath thy azure wings of feathery
    down,
Ribb'd delicate and cloth'd with feather'd gold and
    azure and purple
From thy white shoulders shadowing purity in holi-
    ness.
Thence feather'd with soft crimson of the ruby bright
    as fire
Spreading into the azure wings which like a canopy
Bends over thy immortal Head, in which Eternity
    dwells
Albion, beloved Land : I see thy mountains and thy
    hills
And valleys and thy pleasant Cities.   Holiness to the
    Lord.
I see the Spectres of thy Dead, O Emanation of
    Albion.

This is the song, or rather this is half of the Song of
Los : more need not be quoted, for the end is similar to
the beginning, and quite clearly it is not a song at all.
Los is the spirit of poetry and prophecy incarnate, and
his voice, Blake tells us, is " heard over the whole earth

. . . the Valleys listen silent; the Stars stand still to
hear." What they hear, it must be repeated, is not
song. It is the confused, half-descriptive, half-explana-
tory presentation of a corner of Blake's mystical
scheme, only so far touched with poetry as that the
repetition of such words as lovely, soft, mild, repose,
and an external insistence upon the beauty of the vision
may give it a certain pseudo-poetic atmosphere. " Why
wilt thou rend thyself apart. . . . Come forth O lovely
one " are the only words in which there is so much as a
hint of lyric feeling ; and of the twenty-five lines quoted
there are not more than four that give the least artistic
satisfaction to the uninitiate. Nor, let us observe, can the
passage have any value artistically for the initiate either ;
for explanatory description falls outside the range of
artistic workmanship. If the symbolic system is understood, what can be more tedious, more destructive of
poetry, than to have it explained ? if it cannot be understood without explanation, it is not in condition to be
made the subject of poetry.

A more detailed criticism will become possible to us
as we attempt to make out what Los intends to say.
Jerusalem is that kingdom of art and imagination and
all true religion, to which mankind aspires. " Mild "
and "lovely " are Homeric epithets associated with the
spirit of forgiveness that reigns there. Shiloh, being

L

the spot where the Tabernacle first rested and the religious centre of Israel, may fittingly be identified with Jerusalem, though no new idea is gained by the identification. The significance of the words " of Mount Ephraim " is that it is in the district called Mount Ephraim that you must look for Shiloh on the map. This is neither poetry nor mysticism : it is mere geography ; and as Blake has a mystic geography, we must add that for mystic purposes Shiloh is situated unhappily. Had Blake needed a " correspondence " drawn from the environs of London, he would have chosen Lambeth ; Lambeth being in the south, and therefore suggestive of the " lovely mild " influence from which Jerusalem is born : Shiloh, being north of Jerusalem, has no symbolic value in this context. Here we have at once an example of the laxity to which the mystic poetic method lends itself. It provides no focus, it offers no means of discriminating between what is relevant to say and what is not. The symbols are not clearly related to any objects ; they have no continuity of significance ; they offer no principle by which we can determine whether the words belong to the familiar system we call language, or to a private code. Indeed, as used by Blake, the method provokes the further question, whether the code, not content to be private, is not also inconsistent within itself. Shiloh and Jerusalem,

we seem to be told, are alternative symbols for the
ideal life: they are mild and lovely : Shiloh is situated
upon Mount Ephraim.

The symbolism of the next line appears to be
Biblical, and, if so, needs no special interpretation ;
Blake habitually falls back upon Old or New Testa-
ment imagery when his own ideas give out; the
Bible, as understood by Swedenborg, is the foundation and corner-stone of his myth. Blake passes
on from this to a statement touching the relation of
Jerusalem to Albion, the Sleeping Man. Jerusalem is
Albion's spiritual ideal (Albion standing either for
England or Mankind), an ideal to which he cannot
attain while stretched upon the rocks ; that is, while
his life is bound by an external law. But now to the
idea of Albion, as a man bound to the rock, Blake asks
us to add that of Albion as a country, and to think of
that part of the country in which lie twenty-eight cities,
adjacent to the spiritual realm called Beulah. A beautiful description of Beulah will be found in the opening
of the second book of the *Milton*. Blake's ideal,
Jerusalem, being essentially the ideal of a creative
artist, and representing, I believe, in its central association, the state of mind in which artistic creation
is going forward uninterruptedly, Beulah seems to
correspond to the mental condition, which, though it

involves no elements that confine or violate Jerusalem,
yet falls short of it ; at the same time it is to be regarded as a transitional state, through which the mind
may pass from " Albion " to " Jerusalem." Wordsworth would have called it a " wise passiveness," and
felt it delightful as well as wise.   Blake, in his more
fervid idealism, is moved chiefly to pity by the thought
of it : it is " the pleasant shadow to which all the weak
and weary, like women and children, are taken away as
on wings of dove-like softness."   As to the twenty-
eight cities of Albion, their names are London, Canterbury, York, Ely, Oxford, &c. &c.   They represent, as
Beulah does, states of mind through which Albion
passes on his way to Jerusalem, but their separate
significance is a matter beyond explanation.   The
" Shadow of sleeping Albion " being termed " lovely,"
should, by all the laws of good writing, refer to the
same object as the " lovely mild Jerusalem " earlier
apostrophised, and the " O lovely one " to whom Blake
immediately after appeals.   But Jerusalem is Albion's
Emanation, whereas his Shadow is his Body : thus the
word " lovely " is used not to any artistic or mystical end,
but merely because the mood in which Blake is writing
demands the introduction of it wherever possible.
Turning aside, then, from his summons to Jerusalem
Blake addresses the Body, and deplores the materialising

tendency in man, which leads to pride, oppression, error and vice—of all of which he makes the city of Babylon his symbol. Yet we may note that the twenty-eight cities among which Albion sleeps, though immaterial as yet, must be made material, must be planted by the sisters (called elsewhere " Beulah's lovely daughters "—we should figure them perhaps as visions which float before the wisely passive, or reposeful, mind) in the bosom of Time and Space's Womb, before they can lead Albion to Jerusalem. In all his references to the material world, Blake reveals this unresolved inconsistency of thought, though he appears to be quite unconscious of it. The remainder of the passage, in which the mystic form of Jerusalem is described, draws nearer to poetry than anything in the preceding lines —partly because there is no intrusion of systematised theory and partly because Blake's many designs, representing Jerusalem allegorically as a figure with six wings (see, notably, the title-page of the book) have familiarised us with the object he is describing and enable us to some extent to enter into the delight to which it inspires him. But, of course, here again, poetically considered, the passage shows a hopeless entanglement of metaphor, and the beauty of an occasional phrase such as

> Thence feather'd with soft crimson of the ruby bright
> as fire

depends not a little upon the relief occasioned by the
momentary appearance in it of a recognisable rhythm
and sense : and, on the other hand, considered mystically
or allegorically, the same metaphorical entanglement is
hardly less a flaw, because there is again no means of
judging which of the images belong to the system and
which are only summoned up by the immediate aspect
of the object described.   Here, in short, as everywhere
in the Prophetic Books, Blake is making the effort to
look through a pair of differently focussed glasses, and,
as a necessary result of the attempt, there is nothing
he sees that is not blurred.

Our analysis of this passage—which may fairly be
taken as typical of Blake's mystic poetising—entitles
us I think to assert that, if it be approached as literature, that is, as one man's thought reduced to universally
intelligible form, it can only be judged vague and pur-
poseless.   Blake had, undoubtedly, a wonderful command of words ; the imitation he made in very early
years of Shakespeare at his most majestic might be
regarded in itself as proving this ; it is an almost
unexampled feat.   But his hold upon the realities, the
experiences, which underlie the use of words and are
the only ultimate support of powerful writing, was
weaker than he knew.   He allowed himself too easily
to suppose that his experiences were of a kind not

expressible in the common language of men, and on
this supposition proceeded to invent a language of his
own for the expression of them. Language, however,
can only exist because one man's mind is, on the whole,
like another man's mind, and because men have, on the
whole, a common knowledge and understanding of the
objects they desire to talk about. Thus the individual
who, having unique experiences, fails to see that the
common tongue is his only vehicle for the description of
them is committing himself to one or the other of two
absurdities, possibly to both. Either he is supposing
his experience to be of such importance to humanity
that it entitles him to impose on all who wish to enter
into it the task of learning a new language ; or he is
forgetting that words are meaningless except in relation
to experiences, and that therefore, if the experience be
indeed unique, he cannot, by merely coining a name
for it, call up its image in any mind but his own.
Now for all Blake's emphatic assertions to the contrary,
the spiritual visions which appeared to him, which he
described in his verses and incorporated in his designs,
were, compared with the objects which present themselves to the normal bodily eye, formless and incom-
plete. The famous " visionary heads " are perhaps too
trivial in conception to be advanced in proof of this ;
but the way in which Blake spoke of them (if we may

trust Gilchrist) seems to show to what a degree of
childishness he could be carried by his belief in the
validity of all that entered or seemed to enter his mind
from every source except the normal. The relapses
into formlessness which occur in many of his completer
imaginative designs are a more important evidence ;
and one may quote also Blake's description of the
mystic converse into which he entered on "the banks
of Ocean" with Homer, Dante and Milton—"majestic
figures, grey but luminous, and superior to the common
height of men."   It is clear that, so far as Blake introduced a systematic scheme of mystical imagery and
nomenclature into his work, he was unwittingly playing
traitor to the imagination which he worshipped and
which was the true source of his poetic and spiritual
insight.   He had a certain theory of life, on the one
hand, and of the place of art in life.   On the other
hand, he had a unique power of memorising, constructing or reconstructing visual appearances.   The exercise
of this was with him so habitual and so instinctive, that
he was able unconsciously to make use of it in order to
obtain a transcendental sanction for the validity of his
theories.   For, as a matter of fact, the entire mystical
mechanism of the Prophetic Books, with its gigantic
dramatis personæ, its geography that violates the laws
of space, its history that neglects the passage of time,

LOS AND THE SUN
BRITISH MUSEUM

To face p. 168

its unexampled fusion of violence and vagueness in almost every department of thought, is a mere fungus of the mind, owing, we must at once add, the luxuriance of its growth to the great vitality, exuberance, and creative power of the individual mind from which it sprang. Everything that Blake tasks this machinery to convey, he conveys more truly and far more incisively in occasional passages where he relapses into terms of common speech ; and, in so far as he believed himself to be doing a poet's or an artist's work in the allegorisation of his ideas, the content of the Prophetic Books themselves is the reply to him. They show the man who, in his sense of lyric appropriateness of speech, ranks with the greatest in our literature, wading knee-deep in a morass of futile terminology, and wasting unique powers of imaginative design in representation of subjects, which, having no recognisable relation to life as men commonly understand and live it, can never carry the full significance of conception he aimed at giving them, can never, except to a small circle of disciples, make any other than the comparatively trivial æsthetic appeal.

CHAPTER IX

THE CONFINES OF POETRY AND PAINTING

BLAKE was a poet as well as an artist, and yet his main interest throughout life was always leading him along the byway of philosophic thought into a land to which neither art nor poetry belongs. This fact gives special importance in the consideration of his work to a question which of itself is most absorbing, the question, namely, how we are to define the difference in a picture between what it represents and what it is, the difference, as more commonly phrased, between its literary and artistic value; the difference, in fact, between a picture and an illustration. The tendency of the general public is to regard all pictures as illustrations merely. The ideal method of despatching a picture gallery on this understanding was given by the American lady, who walked down the centre of the *Salon* with a daughter on each side of her; the daughters consulted their catalogues and identified the pictures by their names; the mother had seen the

picture when she could reply " Oh ! yes." The tendency of the practised critic is to dismiss the illustrative function altogether; he prefers for the most part
to set the so-called " subject " of a picture completely
on one side. Whether Cain is represented in Canaan,
or Joseph of Arimathea among the rocks of Albion, is
to him a wholly insignificant matter. " Here is a
certain collocation of lines or colours ; what is conveyed by them ? what is the meaning of this harmonious
form in the immediate appeal it makes—not to my
knowledge of the Bible—but to my power of penetra-
tive sight ? Is it delightful ? Is it beautiful ? " The
protest is a valuable protest, and yet the position is
reactionary. To know that Cain is Cain and Abel
Abel is not to have seen the picture, although there is
authority as high as Aristotle's for believing that it is
so. You are not very far advanced in the appreciation
of a work of art when you can call the principal figures
by their names ; and you may be able fully to appreciate it without naming them at all. The names,
indeed, are often as irrelevant as the critic thinks they
are ; the picture may be complete without them. As
a rule, however, it is not so ; they generally have their
meaning, and it is generally helpful to true appreciation of a picture to know what this meaning is. In
approaching Blake's work—much of it being on the

confines of painting and poetry—it is essential to have as clear as possible a view of the various ways in which these two sides of the art are interwoven.

It may be premised that Blake himself was quite unconscious of the problems we are desiring to approach. The appreciation he has commanded in recent years has come to him mainly from a school of critics who tend to pursue beauty as an abstraction. Blake, just because he was an artist born, bothered his head very little about that. It was the intellectual side of art, art as a medium for the presentation of "immortal thoughts," which engrossed his conscious effort. If it could have been proved to him that these thoughts were an irrelevancy, the entire fabric of his art, as he himself understood it, must have been overthrown. One of his greatest works is *Sir Jeffrey Chaucer and the Nine-and-Twenty Pilgrims on their journey to Canterbury;* his object in executing it is, as he narrates at length, to follow Chaucer's conception down to the minutest of details, and half the greatness of his picture depends on the quite miraculous success with which this object is achieved : its power, as Blake himself mentions, is the power of the poetic visionary. In later years, when he engraved his *Illustrations to the Book of Job,* Blake was as lavish in the use of explanatory texts and mottoes as Ruskin himself could have

been ; and the main work of his life was the production of books, in which the text itself was an engraving,
and of which it is often a chief difficulty to decide
whether the designs are an accompaniment to the
words or the words to the designs.

The subject we are embarked on is so complicated
and has so many sides of possible approach that we
may perhaps save time and energy by taking a head-
long leap into the midst of it.   One of Blake's most
characteristic and most daring achievements is a colour-
print, in the possession of Mr. Graham Robertson,
known as the *Pity*.   The theme is taken from *Macbeth*,
and is a theme which it may safely be asserted no artist
but Blake could have ever dreamed of treating pic-
torially.   Prostrate upon the ground, her hair mingling
with the grass, is the form of a woman—a mother :
in the air above, two spectral horsemen, mounted on
blind, lurid, fantastic steeds, rush by at whirlwind
swiftness, one of them stooping from the saddle, as he
passes, to catch and carry off her child.   Quite apart
from any meaning it may have, the various forms and
characters in the picture are treated in such a way as
to produce at once a quite gorgeous impression of
imaginative recklessness.   In the tossing of the hair
upon the wind, in the splendid stride of the horses, in
the frank and simple opposition of the tempestuous

energy of speed above, the intensive energy of conflict below, in all these things there may well seem enough for the spirit of artistic appreciation to repose on. But to enjoy them in their true bearing we need to consider more accurately what purpose the artist had in making a collocation so strange. The lines illustrated occur in that speech of Macbeth in which he is counting over to himself the possible consequences of Duncan's murder :

> This Duncan
> Hath borne his faculties so meek, hath been
> So clear in his great office, that his virtues
> Will plead like angels, trumpet-tongued, against
> The deep damnation of his taking off :
> And pity, like a naked new-born babe,
> Striding the blast, or heaven's cherubim, hors'd
> Upon the sightless couriers of the air,
> Shall blow the horrid deed in every eye,
> That tears shall drown the wind.

These reckless riders are the cherubim ; this naked babe is a similitude of Pity : but clearly to call the whole picture *Pity* is to suggest nothing but a travesty of its true theme : there is no more of pity in it than there is in the words and disposition of Macbeth. The word pity is made use of and an image suggested which must move to pity if anything can move to it ; but the entire current of Macbeth's feeling is in a contrary

sense; and Blake merely accepts the image to use it
as a mirror to the feeling, and by the very refusal of
pity to enhance horror and apprehension.   The theme
is not *Pity* at all, but the Furies, the trackers of murder,
as they present themselves to the mind of their victim.
This is what the picture *represents*, and represents convincingly.   If any one should ask further what it *is*,
perhaps we may answer that it is the reflex of Blake's
almost delirious delight in the magnificent vividness
and inconsequence of Shakespeare's metaphor.

If this analysis is correct it would seem to follow
that a picture does not necessarily lose by being an
illustration, although naturally it does lose by being
supposed the illustration of an idea it never was intended to illustrate at all.   For this picture, which is
one of the most forcible Blake ever conceived, is simply
a pictorial variation upon a theme supplied by Shakespeare : deprived of its relation to that theme, presented
to the mind as a completely independent work of art,
it would only appear a pure extravaganza.   To appreciate truly those qualities in it which make their appeal
directly to the eye, it is necessary to provide them
with an atmosphere, to see them in the light of certain
ideas they presuppose.   Another example may make the
point still clearer.   One of Blake's smaller engraved
books is called *The Gates of Paradise :* it consists of a

short poem, one of the most enigmatic he ever wrote,
and of about a score of engraved allegorical designs,
themselves hardly less enigmatic than the verse, and
very sketchy in execution. As works of art these are
differently estimated—to the present writer they seem
of singularly little value. The interest is in almost
every case in the idea, and this idea is often conveyed
almost as much by the motto under the design as by
the design itself. The frontispiece, for example, represents a clumsy-headed youth, swinging along with outstretched limbs, hat in hand, butterflying ; one butterfly
lies flat upon the ground before him, another soars
away among the trees: and the butterflies are not
butterflies, but human children. We are such children, apparently, in the rude hands of fate: for we
find appended the motto "What is man?" Or in
another design a pallid caterpillar, clinging to the edge
of a dark oak leaf, bends over a hardly less pallid
chrysalis cradled upon an oak-leaf below : and this
chrysalis has a human head, so that one might imagine
a baby in its swaddling clothes, only that the face is
not a baby's face but the face of a mature man, with
all the insipidity of self-satisfaction that only maturity
can bring. " Alas ! " the motto reads, and the whole
intention becomes plain—man prisoned and contented
in his prison, man whose true destiny is something so

much nobler.—" Ah ! weak and wide astray, ah ! shut in narrow doleful form ! " Later, when Blake reads Dante, he detects a new significance for his parable and adds the lines

noi siam verme
Nati a formar l'angelical farfalla.[1]

In short a work of pictorial art does not necessarily explain itself. The same is true of a painting as of a poem. In few poems does the poet say everything that he wishes his hearers to understand : he gives out a subject, and trusts them to supply his treatment of it with a foundation or background out of the stock of common human experience. Painting, because of the nature of the medium it employs, is even less explicit, and therefore must rely more than poetry on the understanding which its public brings to it. It would be a mistake to suppose that the understanding thus supplied is necessarily supplied from alien regions of the mind : it makes little difference where it comes from : one picture will presuppose one kind of knowledge or susceptibility, another another. A picture may illustrate a poem, but it may also illustrate, explain, or prepare the way for another picture.

Blake's series of illustrations to the Book of Job exemplifies this in a variety of ways, but there is a particular

---

[1] Worms are we, born to make the angelic butterfly.

interest in considering the relation of the decorative borders to the designs themselves. Some of Blake's finest work, his peculiar pictorial gift at its highest, is lavished upon these borders. In theory they are mere flowers of the fancy, a kind of living embroidery, twined round the main column of thought; and these columns, as first conceived and executed, stood without them. A chief part of their purpose is to give occasion for the display of the texts appropriate to the various subjects in hand, and the simplicity implied in this is a great part of their charm. But they are full of ideas, full of beauty, and often enhance wonderfully both the significance and the beauty of the central design. It is of the highest interest to watch the various ways in which their decorative and associative function is made use of. One of the most complex in significance is the border to the twelfth design. The design is, of course, complete without it; and the series as a whole presupposes a close acquaintance with the Book of Job, so that the texts are a piece of added grace on Blake's part. But the border is essentially the border to this design and to no other. Let me suggest a few of the more obvious of the ideas that went to its construction. In the first and last designs, the peace and quietude of the nomadic pastoral life is suggested in the borders by the form of a simple over-arching tent.

That theme is here repeated under variation : thus we
cannot understand this twelfth design unless we have
seen and understood the first : to appreciate the
variation, the theme must be clearly present in your
mind. The outline of the tent is supplied by two
flights of joyful figures soaring heavenwards. Below
is the figure of an old man sleeping, to whom appear
two angels and point to these figures, the figures of
his dream. Considered as decoration, this is all help-
fully and sensitively related to the central design ; the
two angels with raised hands are conceived in a delicate subordination to the upright figure of Elihu, and
there is a fine contrast and balance between Elihu,
erect and animated, with bright stars round his head,
and the horizontal form of the old man below him,
subdued to an almost trance-like repose. But the
border only makes its full æsthetic appeal when wider
and subtler ideas are brought to bear upon it, drawn
from our knowledge of what Elihu is saying and from
the relation of this both to the life of Job and to his
present misfortune. Thus considered, all its forms
take on an exquisite suggestiveness. For the tent
which in Job's prosperous times covered him with the
benediction of simplicity, has now in his dark days
taken on wings of inspiration and become a canopy
for the stars. " Lo, all these things worketh God

oftentimes with man to bring his soul from the pit to be enlightened with the light of the living." All this when we have grasped it, we recognise as conveyed æsthetically; but the æsthetic suggestions would have been far too subtle to have been grasped without a clue. Blot out the central design, blot out our knowledge of the Book of Job, erase the texts which Blake has printed in the margins, and half the significance of the border disappears. This may be seen even more forcibly in the framework of the seventh design; more forcibly because what seemed true only of the framework in the case of the *Elihu*, is equally true here of the design itself. For here the design requires its border not a whit less than the border implies the design. Without the sorrowful resignation and tranquillity of the two seated forms above, the obstreperous violence of gesture with which the three friends herald their approach, instead of being painful merely, would be quite intolerable: without the exquisite reminder Blake gives below of the sweet and peaceful associations of the shepherd's life, with its simple outline of hill and clump of trees to give a shade, the burning sky and desolate architecture of the centre-piece would be robbed of half their force. Nor do we in the least leave the province of the art-critic strictly so-called, if we refer the value of this opposition to the idea in which it originated, and describe it as representing the patience of Job and its promise maintained in the very extremity of his affliction. " Ye have heard of the patience of Job and seen the end of the Lord." A different kind of conception underlies the relation of design to border in the tenth number of the series. The border here is of very little significance æsthetically, except as carrying on a decorative principle which has been laid down in earlier numbers and so securing continuity. Its purpose is symbolic; Blake gives in the margin his criticism of the behaviour of Job's friends. Chains are a conspicuous item, and the leaves of the " indignant thistle whose bitterness is bred in his milk ; " while the foreground is occupied by contrasting figures of the eagle and the owl.

> The owl that calls upon the night
> Speaks the unbeliever's fright.

" When thou seest an eagle thou seest a portion of genius. Lift up thy head." Adversity, as Blake elsewhere observes, is the main test of friendship; it is when a man's success deserts him that

> All his good friends show their private ends
> And the eagle is known from the owl.

In the seventeenth number, for which Blake's feeling is deeply and intimately enlisted, the Psalms and Epistles are quoted in the upper margin, and in the lower an angel points to a scroll and two open testaments, on which are inscribed Blake's favourite passages from the Gospel of St. John: even more moving—in the foreground of the wonderful eighteenth design, which represents Job doing sacrifice for his friends, Blake introduces his own tools and palette, in mute obeisance to that spirit of forgiveness which had been the inspiration of his life.

To those who are interested in the various methods of symbolic, literary, and purely artistic presentation, these borders offer a quite absorbing study, and the intermingling of methods is not, it should be remarked, confined to them. The fourth design of the series presents in itself a rich example of complicated suggestiveness. From the æsthetic point of view, a main feature of interest, as Mr. Binyon has remarked, is the effect of desperate swiftness obtained by setting the two runners to run opposite ways ; and this effect is enhanced further by the peaceful nonchalance of the ram and the two sheep grazing. But another kind of interest belongs to the picture considered symbolically. It is transitional, and represents Job's passage from prosperity to misfortune. The Gothic cathedral, with

the quiet hill under which it stands, and the light in
the sky behind it, is vanishing from the arena ; lowering
clouds twist and coil overhead.   Job, his flocks about
him, sits under the shade of a green tree, but immediately behind rise the heavy " Druidical " stones,
which Blake makes prominent in his landscape all
through the period of Job's affliction.   There is a
shady wood in the background and green grass over the
earth ; nothing like these appears again before the
eighteenth design.   This alternation of light and darkness is used also as an æsthetic effect ; but the wood, a
symbol of light, joins for æsthetic purposes with the
powers of darkness, while the Druid stones are in the
light.   In the framework the interweaving of method
is even bolder ; in the lower part, roots and tortuous
flame, and a bent fragment, half limb, half bough, give
vague forewarnings of pain and misery to come ; in the
upper, the figure of Satan among clouds " going to
and fro in the earth and walking up and down in it "
is sketched with the severest economy of line but with
the very height of pure artistic effect, while the two
figures prostrate before him, that droop over the upper
angles of the design—a very miracle of ingenuity—are
the first use of a decorative theme which Blake continues to employ with exquisite variation all through
the series.

Pictures, in short, according to Blake's idea of them, require a programme : the principle of pure æsthetic criticism is one that is inapplicable to the main part of his work. There are probably very few artists to whose work it can be applied exclusively. Of all arts painting is the most dependent for its appeal upon associations which, as painting, it can do little or nothing to suggest. To reject these associations, to treat them as if, because not the essential of the art, they are therefore irrelevant or obscuring, is to commit the gravest of errors. The pure artistic impulse, the impulse to express thought and feeling through form and colour appealing only to the eye, was certainly the deepest impulse of Blake's mind : it is so deep he never questions it, so deep that he can in his theory sever it from the whole field of its natural exercise, while still in his practice maintaining it alive. And yet he was only able thus to sever it because it was, to his mind, essentially a means to an end, a vehicle for the transmission of an independent reality, the servant of the idea. His ideal in art " to cast out everything that is not imagination," if applied strictly to painting, ought to have led him to the severest unity of conception, to that almost musical employment of its medium which the æsthetic critic demands. But imagination, as he applied it to the concrete, always

"MYSTERY"
BRITISH MUSEUM

carried with it a reference to something which lay behind both poetry and painting, something in fact which was common to the whole of art—the material of life itself. His artistic impulse urged him to testify to the truth and the desirableness of a certain kind of spiritual attitude which could not in its essentials be regarded as a thing manifesting itself to the eye. And at best his effort was to translate this into terms of visual experience, to use the eye as an interpreter. Thus it comes about that there is often a line of division to be drawn between the meaning of his pictures and their beauty. In a perfect picture, its meaning is its beauty, and you need say no more about it : Blake's are sometimes beautiful in spite of their significance, sometimes significant without being beautiful at all, sometimes so beautiful that it almost ceases to matter whether they are significant or not.

I could cite no better example of my meaning than the illustration on the opposite leaf. The motive of the design is of a complexity that only Blake could have conceived. A vast sunflower opens like a lily upon the surface of the sea ; seated upon it, as upon a throne, the form of a woman, winged and crowned; for canopy to her throne a shell with sun and moon and stars contained within it. Light shines in her and from behind her; her shell, in which the sun and moon show dim, is itself a beacon gleaming out over dark waters. Looking at her wings again we do not know that they are wings, nor whether she has two or four or six: they are become falling water, and her knees the rocks of the waterfall, and her flower the fountain basin with petals for overflow; while she, in the midst, is Loreley, mysterious, impassive, dreaming among her streams. Above her, her hair rises like living flame and her golden crown floats fourfold like a benediction over her head. In composing these exquisite complexities of evanescent form, Blake was not delighting in form for its own sake. To prove this it is enough to point to the circles which represent sun and moon; they have their value as circles in the design, but that would not have sufficed to secure them their place in it. A pair of threepenny bits would not have fulfilled Blake's purpose. The sun and moon are there to call up an idea. We are to connect them with the shell in the hollows of which they are placed, and by their means to recognise it as the "blue mundane shell," as a symbol, that is, of the material universe. Blake came, clearly, to his symbolic use of this expression by a hint from the shape and colour of the sky over our heads;

we see this in the lovely passage in *Milton*, where the
lark mounts

Upon the wings of light into the great expanse,
Re-echoing against the lovely blue and shining
heavenly shell.

Of course the sky, if it is like a shell at all, is
like a cockle-shell, not like a periwinkle; and, to
analyse more acutely, it was the idea of a shell as a
covering, not as a form, which prompted Blake to the
metaphor; when, on first arriving at Felpham, he feels
himself more closely in touch with spiritual things, he
expresses his delight by saying that " now begins a new
life, because another covering of earth is shaken off."
In the same sense the sky is a shell, imprisoning his
soul; something to which, like the lark, it aspires, but
only that it may penetrate and pass beyond it.   But
nothing of this is suggested in Blake's gorgeous periwinkle, which, from the pictorial point of view, is a
symbol gone astray.   As picture, its value is that its
point makes an admirable chimney, and that its wings
fall harmoniously—perhaps, indeed, too harmoniously
—into line with the drooping fountain wings below.
As for the sunflower, it means, of course, what it
always meant to Blake after he had written his immortal lyric in the *Songs of Experience*, the spirit

weary of the bonds of the flesh. Why here it takes the habits of the water-lily is a knotty problem harder to untie;—perhaps the shell required sea; perhaps, rather, the leading motive of weariness and despondency naturally suggested a waste of waters for its background. Like these shapes attendant on her, the central figure has also her precise symbolic meaning. Different interpreters would probably attach her to different parts of Blake's scheme. Messrs. Ellis and Yeats identify her as " the mixture of love and jealousy called by the female Religion, as Vala, the triple crowned, being also Rahab, and Babylon, or Mystery." Blake no doubt intended her for something at least as complicated and at least as unintelligible as this. It need not trouble us, however, to discover exactly what she stands for; it would be a matter of a year's study before we could be sure we were in the right. Blake is illustrating his allegory, and his allegory is an allegory of the human soul. The sunflower and the mundane shell suggest to us symbolically in what relation the soul is to be viewed. She is born to aspiration, and all the beauty of heaven and earth are around her; and yet this beauty shuts her in. There is the mystery which, weary, like the sunflower, of time, she contemplates in her despondent languor, to which her closed eyes tell us she can discover no reply. This is Blake's condemnation of

those who love Nature, who are held in the toils of
earthly beauty,—his representation of the one problem
he recognised everywhere in life.

> Why, if the Soul can fling the Dust aside,
> And naked on the Air of Heaven ride,
>   Were't not a Shame—were't not a Shame for him
> In this clay carcase crippled to abide?

He sees that shame, and, for himself, he will have none
of it. " There is no Natural Religion." " Nature is the
work of the Devil." " Another sun feeds our life's
streams, we are not warmèd with thy beams." All
earthly beauty, and earthly sustenance is a temptation
and a snare; then why, why are we bound down to it?
" Why cannot the ear be closed to its own destruction
or the glistening eye to the poison of a smile?" It is
the eternal problem. Inexplicable beauty, inexplicable
sadness haunt one another in the marvellous design of
which these ideas were the inspiring motive. The
design is the child of the ideas, and yet as a design, as
a picture, it does not express them, it presupposes them
already known, and known so well that they may be
played with. Of course this is an extravagant claim ;
perhaps no artist but Blake would have been guilty of
the amazing self-absorption implied in it ; but the rich
suggestiveness of the completed work justifies whatever

liberties he may have taken in its conception. For the whole is like some rare gorgeous flower, or as if the queen of ocean had risen, her living canopy about her, to brood and blossom upon the surface. And thus what it means is of comparatively little moment, because it is alive; because it means far more than by any code of symbolism we could ever extract from it.

All through Blake's work the unconscious battle between expression and symbolism goes on. In his poetry symbolism easily conquered; in his design the fight was drawn. The pitfalls of symbolism are more readily discoverable in painting than in poetry. A collection of symbols, as the painter would be driven to display them, could not fail to declare itself in its true nature—a mere box of tools; at the least, he will have to make them decorative and presentable, and the realities of his art will thus of necessity obtrude themselves. But this helpful reminder, which the painter draws from his enforced commerce with the mere appearances of things, is balanced by a drawback that comes from the same source and occasions much confusion. The painter can only express over a basis of representation. He wishes to paint " Joy," he cannot do so. All he can do is to paint forms more or less irrelevant to his purpose, and to paint them in such a way that joy may, in or through them, become visible.

The Argument

I loved Theotormon
And I was not ashamed
I trembled in my virgin fears'
And I hid in Leutha's vale!

I plucked Leutha's flower,
And I rose up from the vale;
But the terrible thunders tore
My virgin mantle in twain

PLUCKING THE FLOWER OF JOY
BRITISH MUSEUM

To face p. 190

On what principle, then, is he to decide how much of the form and what elements in it are needful to convey the emotion? This is one of the unanswered problems of the art. In its highest forms, painting, like all art, aims at making matter a vehicle for the transmission of feeling; but it is haunted more than any other by questions as to the true relative positions of the two. In Blake's work the problem appears in its intensest form; he was all for feeling, and yet he recognised the human figure, by preference the nude, as the highest vehicle for his artistic expression. He looked on the material world as a nonentity; yet his artistic ideal bound him to it hand and foot. It is in vain he draws a sunflower to express aspiration after the infinite; he expresses nothing of the kind: nor does he add to its expressiveness by being so far neglectful of the form that we mistake what he has drawn for a sea-anemone. What is true of the mere symbol is not less true of the more direct representation. The artist who wishes to depict horror, and chooses the nude as his vehicle, does not achieve his purpose by distorting the frame past recognition; he has depicted not horror, but chaos— his own ignorance, in short. The more highly organised the form, the acuter becomes the problem. Blake constantly takes astounding liberties, and justifies them; he draws the figure with one leg shorter than the other, or with only one leg instead of two ; he introduces impossible simplifications of outline, impossible complexities of movement, often with complete success. Yet the greatest figure artists have not shown this kind of disrespect for their material, and that it is half weakness in Blake is proved by the fact that, though often successful in the use of this kind of liberty, he far more often fails. Among his nudes are numbered some of the worst atrocities ever committed in the name of Art. Yet his occasional successes suffice to reveal the importance of the problem. To what extent are material conditions to be received as binding ? Are the muscles of the body to be regarded as numerable or not ? By an artist such as Blake the material form is not pursued for its own sake, it is merely the outward visible sign of an inward spiritual state ; that inward state is what he really wishes to put on canvas. Is the relative length of arms or legs of any moment so long as the final spiritual truth appears ?

All that can be called certain—put by the practice of great masters out of doubt—is that none of these questions admits of an unqualified reply. Blake's claim for painting, that " it exists and exults in immortal thoughts," is a true one. The painter paints immortality. His eye is on the spiritual world. " But,

"THE BILLOWS OF ETERNAL DEATH"

CAPTAIN ARCHIBALD STIRLING

To face p. 192

then, so is mine, so is yours." What is more important
to note is that his only concern is with appearances.
Appearance is his reality. If a man is shooting
through the sky at comet-speed, the effect will probably be to elongate his legs; if he is stretching one
arm out of heaven to set a compass to the earth, we
shall not wish to ask what he is doing with the other;
he is a one-armed man for us; just as, were he spinning
like a Catherine-wheel, he might rightly be represented
with five arms or with six. Many of Blake's liberties
are the result of his instinctive recognition of this kind
of imaginative truth. The examples quoted are of the
crudest description; but then Blake's imagination often
landed its puppets in queer predicaments. The principle, to be fully understood, needs to be worked out
minutely in its details. Among Blake's loveliest inventions is the well-known frontispiece to the *Songs of
Experience*, reproduced in Gilchrist's *Life*. Does the
intense repose and quietude of the horizontal figures
conceal, or is it conveyed by, the fact that they are
between seven and eight feet in length? We need
hardly be at pains to inquire. They might be ten feet
long, and we could only be grateful for the added
feet of beauty. The error in representation is lost
sight of because of the perfection of sympathy in the
expression. Clearly there is no standard of the relativity

N

of form to feeling to be arrived at by any external method of consideration. The shape and quality of objects is modified by the atmosphere in which they appear to us. Emotion provides such an atmosphere. The artist, like the lover, being all compact of imagination, sees " Helen's beauty in a brow of Egypt," and what he sees he paints.

To Blake, the human figure was the ultimate symbol of a divine reality. Yet it was only a symbol; something more august than itself was behind it: it was still mere malleable clay. Thus he did not falsify his deepest conviction when, in his art, he frankly treated it as subservient to the artistic design. The lesser natural forms are commonly treated thus by artists of all times and schools ; but in our Western art it is usual to regard the human figure as a thing apart, and to treat the design as secondary to the figures which form part of it, to be realised by means, rather than in defiance, of the limitations Nature has imposed. This is merely a convention, but temperance and prudence have contributed to its establishment, and the freedom, which results from disregarding it, has its dangers as well as its delights. A law is, in fact, only the more exacting when it is unformulated. The moment the conventional understanding is suspended, we become aware that a far loftier ideal of artistic and organic

MAN IN THE CHARIOT OF NATURE

CAPTAIN ARCHIBALD STIRLING

unity comes into view, that the artist who sets out to play with Nature's noblest organism can only justify his daring in the creation of forms equally perfect in balance and significance.   The highly characteristic and impressive design on the page opposite will exemplify the ideas I have in view.   It portrays, we are told, Regenerate Man, enthroned upon the chariot of Nature, the lion and serpent subdued to serve him.   A hundred other complex symbolic suggestions will be discoverable by the enthusiast.   We need not now decipher them.   But it will be interesting to ask whether the forms, whatever ideas they may be intended to convey, are satisfactorily unified.   In this curious medley has the imagination fulfilled its own ideal?   It is difficult, at first, not to be over-influenced by the very boldness of the conception.   If the Lamb is the triumph of Blake's poetry, the Serpent is the triumph of his design, and he has nowhere asked more complicated service of it than here.   The wheel is masterly: the problem of its continuity solved, as so much is solved, by relegation to the space beyond the frame. But what of the junction of shaft and wheel? and of the shaft itself?   Under the utmost stretch of sympathy these could not be pronounced successful.   The wheel, for all its material unreality, is a rolling wheel: the shaft is neither snake nor wood, it is merely a piece of

mottled nonsense. This holds even more forcibly of
the pirouetting unicorn contrivances that rise from the
human heads of these lion-chargers, rooted apparently
each in a pineapple. There is only one way of taking
these in which they become even tolerable—when the
two heads are amalgamated and the horns treated as a
natural pair. Such a feat is, unfortunately, made impossible by the contrasting expressions which Blake has
placed upon the countenances of his steeds. The mild
ingenuous vacuousness of the more distant of the two
might have gone far to render him credible as a creature fitted for the peculiar cart, harness, postillion and
other paraphernalia we see him here provided with : but
the stage truculence of his companion's upturned eye-
brow, though it perhaps does something to explain the
rigid action of his forefeet, raises too prominently the
question, what this pair of Nebuchadnezzars can be
about ? It is not difficult to see how Blake arrived at
his conception. The effort, quite clearly, was to combine
the human features with the leonine : the forehead is to
harmonise with the mane : this however does not make
the human expression less ridiculous, and does nothing
to relieve the absurdity of the contrast between the one
head and the other : if the first is the lion, the second
is perhaps Livingstone ? At any rate we have here a
clear case of the dangers that are likely to ensue when

Their strength, or speed, or vigilance, were given
In aid of our defects. In some are found
Such teachable and apprehensive parts.
That man's attainments in his own concerns
Matchd with th'expertness of the brutes in theirs
Are oft times vanquishd and thrown far behind.

Cowpers Task
Bᵏ VI.

ADAM AMONG THE ANIMALS
BRITISH MUSEUM

To face p. 197

the human form or parts of it are placed in purely imaginary contexts. It is not convention, merely, that revolts when a serpent's body is made to terminate in a human hand. There is certainly nothing beautiful in such a combination : and as for meaning, a hand has far too much and the coils of a serpent's body far too little, for any true fusion of them to be possible : part, too, of the horror, or meaning, of a serpent's body is that it is body and hand in one. Worse still is the combination of human with animal features. Such combinations may have some symbolic value ; but in artistic effect they can hardly fail to be barbarous. The animal form has its own proper anguage and expression, a language severely limited in scale : and the human features, if they are to harmonise with it, must somehow be induced to part with their natural complexity of significance. Exactly so far as they remind us of all that a man has it in him to be, we shall be shocked, when we see animals carrying them, by the incongruity of the ideas they summon up. Thus, though the pursuit of natural form, however faithful, brings no assurance of artistic achievement, departure from it, unless in obedience to a principle equally perfect in sensitiveness and vitality, can end in nothing but disaster. There is nothing inherently impossible or ridiculous in the task which Blake has set himself in this design: it is full of imaginative conquests, and brilliant feats of daring. Yet the territory as a whole has not been finally subdued.

The fact is that Blake made himself far too much at ease in the realms of imagination. It was part of his theory that the effort of creation, to be perfect, must be spontaneous. He considered the critical and reflective faculties as of inferior origin, and would have thought it a desecration of his work to have brought them to bear upon it. But it is very rarely that a conception presents itself to the artist complete in all its details. There is a mass of Blake's work in which his treatment of the figure is merely manneristic. The imaginative effort is concentrated on seizing and representing a particular effect of movement or crisis of emotion. Everything else is disregarded. Groups of figures are treated with as little ceremony as leaves on a tree. They curve one way or another in response to the demands of symmetry, or in a vague extravagance of sympathy with the central idea. They have no separately imagined identity. They are not thought out. Some of Blake's most distressing tricks grew upon him as the result of this perfunctory method. In many of his more careless nudes, the legs do not leave the body as legs at all: the effect is as if the trunk had first been imagined continuous,

like a snake's, and afterwards divided. This is a singularly repulsive trait. Hardly less so, in the draped
figures, is the trick of providing them, back view, with
a broad pleat which starts at the nape of the neck and
continues in an unbroken curve to the ground. There
is a picture of the Ascension in which all the Apostles
are habited in this style. To the secular mind an
uncomfortable suggestion occurs of newts or even tad-
poles. Worse still is the conventionalised anatomy
to which Blake often gives artificial prominence under
these sheet-like garments. It is relevant to notice here
these terrible defects, because Blake could never have
suffered from them had he not been beset by a peculiarly
exalted pictorial ideal. He wanted a picture to be
itself, to represent nothing but its subject : and the
subject, in his eyes, was the feeling of those who partici-
pated in the scene, their feeling as individuals relative to the central idea, and their collective feeling as
the medium through which the idea itself was to be
expressed. But how, with this ideal before him, could
he expect to cover every inch of the ground with
minutely organised detail while yet portraying nothing
but what was significant ? Artists, as a class, are content to accept the fact that a man has two legs as in-
evitable and make the best they can of it. If a man
has nothing else to do with his legs, he can at least be

made to stand upon them. Blake would not have this. All the parts must show a direct emotional interplay. Every touch must tell, and the same theory which sometimes led him to elaborate the figure into a map of imaginary muscles led him, at others, to disregard its most elementary material claims. The design overleaf aptly illustrates this method and its results. What Blake intended by it will not be clear except to the initiate. His German interpreter reproduces it under the title, *The Holy Family*. The prominently symmetrical distortion to which the figures of Joseph and Mary are subjected makes this error pardonable. Little appears in it to the unaided eye except an intolerable crudity of design, only matched by the general insipidity of the forms and imbecility of expression on the features. Blake, the artist, sank, it must be admitted, sometimes even lower than this. But there are few more actively displeasing compositions to be found in the range of his thoughtfully executed work. The fact is, that from the mystical point of view he had much here to express, and was thus peculiarly disdainful of the mere mundane forms of things. *Christ in the Lap of Truth* is his theme, and the rigid symmetry of the design is a conscious or unconscious expression of the nature and quality of truth itself. Christ's relation to the Truth is summed up for Blake in the Crucifixion :

CHRIST IN THE LAP OF TRUTH
W. GRAHAM ROBERTSON, ESQ.

To face p. 201

hence the outstretched arms, and the anguish upon the
Virgin's face.   "And Jesus said : 'Thus do men in
Eternity one for another, to put off by Forgiveness
every sin. . . . Wouldest Thou love one who never
died for Thee or ever die for one who had not died for
Thee? And if God dieth not for Man and giveth not
himself eternally for Man, Man could not exist, for
Man is Love, as God is Love.'" The same spirit of
forgiveness is typified in the figures of the child and
lamb below.   It is easy to indicate these main threads
of idea : not so easy to convey the depth of hold they
had upon the artist's mind.   The inspiration of his life
is in them; and the nobility of that inspiration has
passed into his rendering of Truth, of the Virgin, and
of the Christ Child.   But the four remaining figures are
bare decorative adjuncts; what feeling they convey is
of the most conventional description.   In ill-constructed
buildings one sometimes sees the shape of a window
painted upon the brickwork for appearance' sake, presumably to remind spectators of certain principles of
symmetry which the architect has failed to incorporate
in his design.   The symmetry of Blake's angels has an
equivalent effect.   His imagination falters because his
ideas are exhausted, and he falls back helplessly on his
belief in the grand effect of " unbroken lines, unbroken
masses," with a pitiable result.   He does not see that

there can be no symmetry between the figures of
Joseph and Mary, because the one is luminous with
thought and feeling, the other a mere accessory.
The artist's problem is to fill his frame with a just
balance not of shapes, but of ideas. For all his theorising Blake has never really faced this as a fact. And
the effect of the error is intensified by his high artistic
ideal; by the fact that he has accustomed us to view
his figures in relation to an animating emotion.

The fecundity of Blake's imagination often led him
into still more serious errors. In his foreword to
the illustrated edition of *The Grave*, Fuseli remarked
with justice that the execution of the artist "sometimes excites our wonder, and not seldom our fears,
when we see him play on the very verge of legitimate
invention." Blake was, of course, wholly unaware that
legitimate invention had a verge. The illustrations
to *The Grave*, which excited Fuseli to fear and
wonder, are mild; yet they raise many problems for
criticism. The conception of *The Soul hovering over
the Body reluctantly parting with Life* is of great
beauty : and because an exquisite sensitiveness and
suggestiveness of treatment pervade the work (the
open window and wide landscape with calm evening
sky are in subtlest harmony with the theme) the
symbolic representation of the soul as a woman is

not questioned. But when in another print, we see
the Soul, again as a woman, " exploring the recesses
of the grave," the entire absence of design, the utter
disconnectedness of Soul below and Body above, the
hideous and lifeless mannerism displayed in the figure
of the Body, combine to reduce the painter's symbolical
devices to an offence, and to convince us that, whatever
the Soul is, it is never a curious woman prying with a
candle into dark corners. A great part of the artist's
gift is in the power to distinguish subjects capable
of pictorial presentment from subjects incapable of it.
Blake's enthusiastic championship of painting, his
call for a wider field for the exercise of creative
imagination, led him, as his other enthusiasms led
him, to degenerate at times into a mere theorist, and
robbed him of this distinguishing power. " Weaving
the winding-sheet of Edward's race," he cries out,
fired by reading Gray's *Bard*, " is a bold and daring
and most masterly conception. . . . Poetry consists
in these conceptions ; and shall Painting be confined
to the sordid drudgery of facsimile representations of
merely mortal and perishing substances ? " Oh ! no,
no ! Forthwith he proceeds to paint a picture in which
spirits of murdered bards weave the woof over the
luckless Edward in coils of disembodied blood ; and
this kind of " spiritual " weaving became an accepted

part of his poetic and pictorial stock-in-trade. He fails to see that as a pictorial *motif* it is worse than meaningless. There are certain images which language rightly can rely on for the simple reason that the mind is not called upon to realise them visually; to represent them in painting is merely to rob them of their suggestiveness, to thrust before the mind all the qualities in which they are unlike the object. Blake's illustrations to Young's *Night Thoughts* teem with childish errors of this description: he even sinks so low as to conceive that spiritual grandeur can be expressed in feet and inches.

The illustration opposite exemplifies a similar misunderstanding at its height. The subject is the Four-and-twenty Elders casting their crowns before the throne of God and before the Lamb. Blake's attempt to draw the four beasts each with six wings about him and full of eyes within has a rather less ridiculous result than one would have expected: more cannot be said. There is a certain dignity of mystery about the original, which the loss of colour in the reproduction takes away. No one would wish to deny that the picture is a highly ingenious piece of devotional pattern-work. But set it imaginatively in relation to the professed subject, and the mind is almost overwhelmed by its grotesque

THE FOUR AND TWENTY ELDERS
W. GRAHAM ROBERTSON, ESQ.

To face p. 204

literality of conception.   In the whole of Blake's work
there is perhaps one more childish feature than the
"book sealed with seven seals"; that is in the
Judgment of Paris, where the hideous sheep-dog
lying at his master's feet has his master's name
inscribed in Greek capitals on his collar.   Such
trivialities and crudities, such lapses into mere
bathos (an almost endless list might be made of
them) have their importance for the critic because
they point to an habitual confusion in Blake's
mind between force and wildness of imagination.
Any idea that came to him when he was "in
the heat of his spirits" was accepted without a
challenge.   The result is at one time as ridiculous
as at another it is sublime.   Very often the peculiarity
of his artistic method suggests a far more abstruse
meaning in his designs than any he intended to convey
by them.   He can at times combine his exuberant
vitality with a remoteness and subtlety of theme so
delicate and so rare that it is incredible to what a
degree he can show himself at other times both lifeless
and commonplace.   Those who find the text of the
prophetic book *Europe* hard of interpretation are
likely to be not less mystified by the illustrations to it.
All kinds of complexities of meaning present themselves to the inquiring mind and are dismissed as

inadequate : it is with a tremor of anticipation that one learns there is a copy of the book in the British Museum in which Blake has himself given the illustrations their names. But the result is a quite painful disenchantment. This gentleman on page 1, whose face is as sharp as his dagger and whose demeanour associates him with the Adelphi, has nothing to do with "Enitharmon's sleep of eighteen hundred years"; he has come from the Adelphi after all; he is simply *The Assassin*, and twenty-seven lines from Ann Radcliffe quoted on the opposite leaf make it clear that the design was suggested by them. *Fire*, *Imprisonment*, *Plague*, *Famine* and *War* are among the other subjects and these, when we recognise them, turn out, every one,[1] to be treated with the utmost crudeness, and extravagance. The figures of *Horror*, *Amazement* and *Despair* on the second page are mere exercises in limb distortion under the inspiration of nightmare, coloured to match. On the third page a female figure who floats horizontally in heaven with hands raised under drooping locks, is mistaken at first sight for an

---

[1] A notable exception is the *Mildews blighting Ears of Corn*, which has little to do with corn and nothing to do with mildew as we ordinarily understand them, but is certainly the most gorgeous study in his favourite spiral curvature that Blake ever turned out.

angel, but the mistake is quickly corrected by an
inscription—

> He like a comet burned . . .
>> And from his horrid hair
> Shakes pestilence and war.
>>> *Milton.*

It may be remarked that as an illustrator of Milton,
Blake was as a rule unhappy.   Though much influenced
by him Blake was aware that Milton was not really a
kindred spirit.   He spoke of Milton as Palladian,
himself as Gothic, and the distinction showed an
admirable insight; but this insight did not prevent
him from ornamenting Milton's Eden with filagree
or from attempting to set the magnificent invisibilities
of Milton's universe before the eye.   No doubt it is
partly because Milton is blind that his range of poetic
vision is so vast :—

> At once, as far as angels ken, he views
> The dismal situation waste and wild . . .

The virtue of his landscape is that it has no outline,
that it is unconfined : like all great artists he produces
his effect as much by what he omits as by what he
expresses; and, on the whole, he omits the very
features on which, if he were a painter, he would be
bound to rely as the necessary framework of his design.

Thus we come back to the problem with which we set out, and are able to ask again more freely how a picture differs from an illustration, or what is the difference in a picture between the literary and the pure artistic idea. It will have been seen with what intensity Blake's work, both in its failures and in its successes, forces these questions upon the mind. All art is illustrative. Poetry was defined by Matthew Arnold as a criticism of life; those understand poetry who understand what poetry treats of—the material with which the poet assumes his readers to be familiar. The same is true of painting. The painter's aim is to enlarge the range of our visionary experience; but he cannot show us more than we have seen already without assuming that we have already seen much. Every picture makes this assumption at the least, and most pictures carry their demands much further. It is an error to suppose that because we have different senses, life can be divided into partitions correspondingly. The nature of things expresses itself completely in every part; the blind and deaf and dumb can each build up a universe and each express their thought in terms intelligible to all. Thus whatever the medium in which the artist works, his purpose and his privileges are ultimately the same. It is never anything less than life itself, and the whole of life, of which he is an interpreter. If he is a painter, his activity is within narrow limits, and he will need to catch at all the aids and props within his reach. No one has ever denied him the right to give a title to his work. The title may be a poem : the aim may be allegorical : the subject a symbol. The work may rest upon ideas, may lead to ideas. All this is so far from disqualifying it that one may safely say that, robbed of these wider references, art would perish of mere inanition. All that needs to be remembered is that these props and crutches, however serviceable they are in substance and however decorative a turn the artist may give to their appearance, are not the essentials of his art. Art in its perfection requires these things to be subsidiary. It is sometimes said that the business of the critic is to consider whether a work is beautiful or not ; to remind the world that, unless it is beautiful, it cannot claim to be a work of art. That however is a point which does not need professional consideration. Beauty, like murder, will out. A far more pertinent part of the critic's business is to discern what crutches an artist makes use of, and why ; to show how they are related to his pure artistic achievement, and to judge whether he justifies his use of them. Blake undoubtedly suffered severely from being a philosopher. It did not improve matters that his philosophy was based on

o

an artistic understanding of life, and was preached
with a passionate one-sidedness of conviction such as
only an artist could command. This did not prevent
him from bringing an external pressure to bear upon
his creative instinct. Yet his work shows convincingly
how much more than the perfect development of eye
and hand must go to the making of a painter ; how
little the abstract pursuit of beauty sums up either the
ideal aims or the actual processes of art ; how wide and
how deep a relation binds the fantasy of line and
colour not only to the kindred fantasies of sound and
language but to all that is most desirable, profoundest,
and most permanent in the life which they interpret
or adorn.

CHAPTER X

BLAKE THE ARTIST

BLAKE, who was so little appreciated in his lifetime, has lately had the good fortune to attract to himself a body of admirers prepared to attach high value to everything that has the mark or seal of authenticity upon it. Within this circle, which includes some distinguished writers, to pronounce a work Blake's is to pronounce it not only interesting but important. Nothing that Blake did, however slight, will be allowed to pass neglected: the work of cataloguing, describing, explaining, the mass of material that has come down to us from his hands is being carried out with a scrupulous and even passionate conscientiousness. One of Blake's most limiting characteristics was his inability to take criticism. "It is easy to acknowledge a man to be great and good," he remarks in *Jerusalem*, "while we derogate from him in the trifles and small articles of that goodness. Those alone are his friends who admire his minutest powers." That kind of admiration

Blake is, in the fullest measure, getting now ; nothing can keep it from him, and his relapse into pathos at the close of his notes to Reynolds's *Discourses*, that "I am hid," which explains much of the virulence of the invective preceding it, is no longer a true expression of his case. Everything that there is to be known about him will be known.

It is not only because the kind of work involved in this exhaustive method is troublesome and fatiguing that the present author has avoided it ; nor even because the results of it would be liable to be tedious to his readers. The enterprise is already embarked on by specialists and critics well equipped for the task of carrying it successfully to its conclusion, and his attitude to the artist disqualifies him from entering into competition with them. In the mass of Blake's work effort, it seems to him, is far more conspicuous than achievement, and much of the effort, he thinks, is misguided and confused ; a minute enumeration of Blake's designs would have in his hands too much of the appearance of a catalogue of failures to represent justly what he believes to be the main truths about Blake's work. Wherever he appears, Blake's rare combination of simplicity and force makes his work, like his ideas, of unusual interest in its bearing upon the central problems of life and art ; and in this connection his failures are quite as significant as his successes. But the attempt to understand their significance is not in any way furthered by counting them. Daring and imaginative as he is, Blake perpetually repeats himself. A small collection of designs, representing his chief varieties of manner in conception and execution, should give us material from which, if we can show proper discrimination in our estimate of the various qualities exhibited in them, we may readily pass to a sympathetic and appreciative understanding of all that he has aimed at or accomplished.

Blake's handicraft divides itself into two branches; there is on the one side his professional work as an engraver, on the other his original creation as an artist. His artistic development brought the two into an intimate and beautiful alliance, his material necessities kept them throughout his life at an enforced interchange. Turning over the collection of loose sheets which are to be seen in the Print Room at the British Museum, we find the frontispiece for *An Elegy* set to music by Thos. Commins, organist of Penzance, Cornwall,

> The shattered bark from adverse winds
> Rest in this peaceful haven finds
> And when the storms of life are past
> Hope drops her anchor here at last . . .

where Blake breaks in upon the measured reserves of
eighteenth-century lament with an intensity of emotion
which is quite bewildering. Yet again he finds occasion
for the exercise of all the grace and delicacy he had
acquired in working after Stothard, to decorate the
announcement of a sale " At Moore and Co's, Manu-
factory and Warehouse of Carpeting and Hosiery,
Chiswell Street, Moor-Fields—the greatest variety of
carpets from the lowest Scotch and Kidderminster,
Wilton and Brussels, to the finest Axminster, Turkey,
and Persia " : Royal Arms appear against a sunset glory
above, with a stately pillar draped in carpet upon
either side ; while, below, the various operations of the
loom are represented in careful detail, a hero and
heroine from Mary Wollstonecraft's stories survey the
establishment, and three pretty fay-like children take
carpets for playthings as if to assure us of the humanity
and gentleness with which their patron carries on his
trade.   These by-products of Blake's versatility, and
offspring of his misfortune, pass, naturally, unrepre-
sented in our illustrations.   But there are hints in
plenty to be gleaned from them both as to what Blake
could and what he could not do, and thus they throw
not a little light upon his more serious and spontaneous
efforts.   One might note, above all, evidence of a
certain bondage to the emotions, which every one must

indeed suspect in Blake from his manner of handling such themes as would justify an essentially passionate treatment. A certain deference arising from the solemnity of these themes leads to a natural hesitancy in expressing the suspicion. The sincerity of the artist's religious belief, the consistent reverence of his intention are everywhere so obvious in his work that a great deal of crudity and extravagance is liable to be passed over as if it sprang from the peculiar imaginative standpoint he takes up. If, in the *Illustrations to the Book of Job*, we are at first sight shocked to find the Almighty depicted as an old man with flowing beard, hardly in his physiognomy distinguishable from Job himself, the error is explained and we condone it because adequate treatment of the theme would clearly be impossible; and the same excuse presents itself when human passion is ascribed to the divine nature. It is difficult for criticism to find any standard for application to these cases; and the result is that serious faults of taste often escape detection, or are even mistaken for merits, through negligent identification of them with the imaginative impetus of the work as a whole. But when the same faults of extravagance and crudity assert themselves in the illustrations to a common fable or a conventional ballad, one cannot be any longer deceived. It must be admitted, on this account,

that to look through Blake's professional hackwork is a
dispiriting affair. The absence displayed in it of so
much as the rudiments of a sense of humour is painful,
and cannot fail to affect our judgment of his serious
work. Because Blake liked laughing, it has been
believed that he had a native fund of wit. But neither
his life nor his work gives any evidence to justify such
a belief. His laughter was of the jovial kind, the
effervescence of animal spirits in unthinking happiness.
It had no tincture in it of intellectual subtlety. Hence
his belief in the virtue of excess, his principle that
"exuberance is beauty," was without an internal cor-
rective, and led him not seldom, even when the feeling
to be expressed was of the most solemn kind, into that
theatrical violence of presentation for which the distinction between triviality and solemnity of circumstance disappears. The attitude of the allegorical
figure which, in the seventh of the designs to Blair's
Grave, represents the Body watching and listening while
the Soul explores the recesses of the grave, is the same
as that of a bather in Hayley's *Ballad of the Dog*, when
he finds himself about to dive into the gaping jaw of a
crocodile.

Blake's chief source of livelihood was his work as an
engraver, and, as engraving was the avenue by which he
made his approach to the temple of art, it would seem

right to give it the first place in attempting a more
systematic exposition of his artistic endowment.
There can be little doubt that Blake's long and arduous
apprenticeship to this most arduous of all the systems
of artistic expression was the means of preserving to
him, in spite of all the thunderbolts of theory he
launched against it, the citadel of his material imagination.   It is a curious fact, at the least, that the
copyist's burin should have been the most familiar tool
in the hands of this apostle of spontaneity, a fact both
curious and, like not a few other prominent facts of
Blake's life, too little allowed for. His imaginative
revels were in part the revels consequent upon release—
though indeed there is little evidence that he resented
or shirked the drudgery of his profession. His passionate belief in imaginative freedom, if it was in part
reactionary, was also both deeply justified by his proved
ability to work under restrictions, and supported by his
constant practice in such work.   But for his regular
employment as an engraver, the lyric spontaneity of his
early designs would probably have followed the same
course as that of the text which they accompanied ;
instead of reaching the climax of his power in the
illustrations to *Jerusalem* and the *Book of Job*, he would
probably have come to lose himself more and more in
wild and vague symbolical complexities. His illustra-

tions to Young's *Night Thoughts*—a comparatively
early work—give us in themselves an inkling of the
course he had it in him to pursue.   It is not surprising
that their publication ceased after the engraving of
forty-three designs, and perhaps Blake's English
admirers should congratulate themselves that the remaining five hundred have found their resting-place
in America.   They need a land larger than ours.   But
to revert ; Blake's skill as an engraver cannot, naturally,
be represented in photographic reproduction ; yet I
have thought it worth while to include among my
illustrations one example of peculiar beauty—engraved
after Sir Thomas Lawrence's pencil sketch of Cowper—
in which, by use of a dotted line, the original effect of
the lead is preserved with unusual faithfulness.   This
plate is sufficient evidence in itself of Blake's power of
perfect accuracy as a copyist and of the refinement of
his sympathy as a translator.   More was sometimes
asked of him.   His drawing after Fuseli of the Egyptian
god Anubis[1] is of a peculiar interest in that its
most expressive feature is not Fuseli's at all but was
supplied to it by Blake himself.   Fuseli, who enjoyed a
scarcely merited reputation, and whose work was passionately extolled by Blake himself, admitted that
Blake was "damned good to steal from"; he also, on

1 Engraved in Darwin's *Botanic Garden.*

WILLIAM COWPER (AFTER LAWRENCE)
BRITISH MUSEUM

To face p. 218

THE FERTILISATION OF EGYPT (AFTER FUSELI)
BRITISH MUSEUM

To face p. 219

more than one occasion, gave his name in public guarantee of the merit of Blake's work. Perhaps it is in return for service rendered that Blake here presents him with the figure of old Nile brooding over his springs. One wonders how often Blake provided, as he here provides, the touch of inventive genius wanting to the artist whose work he professed only to translate. He had bitter feelings on this subject. Perhaps they were better justified than we know. Two other illustrations (pp. 74 and 197) are of interest as showing—with engraving for a medium—various qualities of Blake's design. We may take first that which is also first in chronological sequence, one of the six designs that accompanied Mary Wollstonecraft's *Tales for Children*, published by Johnson in 1791, and lately reproduced in facsimile by the Clarendon Press. Much of Blake's early engraving had been after Stothard, whose influence is here strongly apparent, especially in the child's somewhat simpering features. Blake, it should be added, learned nothing from Stothard which he could not more fruitfully have discovered for himself; but the imitative impulse in him was almost as pronounced as the creative.[1] The more interesting qualities in the

1 There was often violent warfare between them, analogous, perhaps identical, with that described by Blake as waged by imagination against memory. Thus, at a later period, the influence of Titian is such that " when the artist took his pencil to execute his ideas, his

design appear in the pseudo-romantic sentiment of moat
and ruined castle, which forms an apt commentary on
the artificial tone and atmosphere of the text, and in
the fact that the peculiar motive of interlacing tree-
trunks which, as used in the foreground, has an appropriate tenderness and beauty, is twice echoed in the
middle distance with no very recognisable reason or
result; miscalculation of emphasis was one of Blake's
most habitual errors. The same miscalculation and the
same tenderness of touch are equally prominent in the
far more characteristic representation of *Adam among
the Animals,* which was designed and engraved by Blake
some ten years later as a frontispiece to Hayley's
Ballads. There is a rather pretty story told by
Gilchrist to the effect that Blake, when one day viewing the efforts of a not too successful brother artist,
being at a loss how to express himself about them
without sacrifice of truth or courtesy, met his dilemma
with the remark, " Yes, this is what I have been trying
all my life to do, to paint round, and never could."
His interest in modelling and in chiaroscuro generally
was, of course, entirely subordinate to other aims, and,
considering that Blake drew him, one could not call the
power of imagination weakened so much and darkened, that
memory of nature and of pictures of the various schools possessed
his mind, instead of appropriate execution resulting from the
inventions."

Adam of this design particularly flat. Neither his
flatness nor his many other deficiencies are fatal to his
prevailing grace and charm of mien. The lion too is
not a worse lion for being a memory of Albert Dürer,
and the whole design, with its richness of repeated
curve, and its peculiar mingling of formality and sentiment, must be placed with Blake's most interesting,
most piquant inventions. The cock is hit off with
wonderful fidelity to nature ; and what a supernatural
sweep and softness in the peacock's tail ! Regarded as
an example of the engraver's art, this print, which is
contemporaneous with the head of Cowper just referred
to, shows Blake advancing upon his workmanship of ten
years earlier. The obvious crudity of pattern in his
disposition of the lines, notably of the tree-trunks, in
the earlier print may have been due partly to the fact
that his publisher was not asking him for his most
accomplished style. Still they represent a kind of
fault to which the formal school of Basire was naturally over-lenient ; and it is important to note that
the true artistic quality of Blake's engraving continued
to develop to the very end of his days.

Blake's achievement as an engraver was to bring the
mechanics of his trade more and more into sympathy
with his artistic impulse. In the so-called engraved
books—Blake's Illustrated Printing—he followed a free

method of his own invention and showed from the first
a wonderful mastery of his material : but that is
another matter. His early engravings, strictly so-called,
are mannered and hard. Even so late as 1810, when
he engraved his celebrated *Canterbury Pilgrims,* he is a
rigid formalist ; the first impression he creates—despite
the intricacy and originality of his ideas—is of surprise
and even some distaste at the mechanical peculiarities
of method by which he conveys them. The medium is
frankly accepted as a translator's medium, and is not so
used as to become a source of enjoyment in itself. It
was not till he engraved his *Illustrations to the Book of
Job* that Blake ever broke down completely the barriers
which custom had erected between his art and his trade.
His recent work as a wood-cutter may have helped to
give him inspiration. Linnell also brought before his
notice certain works of early Italian engraving by which
he was led to decide on a fundamental revision of his
own method. Thus the plates combine the practice
and experience of a master hand with a trace of
the fresh enthusiastic effort of a novice, and these
qualities, uniting with the fertility of the invention,
the depth of the religious feeling, and with a
certain peculiar intimacy of understanding by which
Blake felt himself both in idea and in experience
related to his theme, have procured for the series

PILGRIMS TO CANTERBURY

BRITISH MUSEUM

To face p. 223

a recognised place among the artistic masterpieces of the world.

The strictures advanced against Blake's earlier method, as seen for example even in his most daring publication the *Canterbury Pilgrims*, are sufficiently explained in the small fragment of this noble design which forms the accompanying illustration. It appeared as the frontispiece of a small book,[1] the text of which was composed of extracts from Chaucer's Prologue, with a translation into modern English, and which would seem to have had no other object than that of bringing Blake's illustration before the public eye. It is not necessary to do more than glance at the disposition of the lines on Chaucer's cloak, to see how little life there is in Blake's distribution of them, how much formality; but if a further inspection should be demanded, we may note that the circular system used in rendering the body of the poet's horse has converted it into a barrel. The original work from which this engraving was taken is one of the most remarkable exhibitions Blake ever gave of pure imaginative power, and one of the few pictures in which his theory at once fulfils and justifies itself in his practice. "Minute organisation" is here, expressing and not destroying "character": here too are the "unbroken

---

[1] "The Prologue and Characters of Chaucer's Pilgrims, intended to illustrate a particular design of Mr. William Blake," published 1812.

lines, unbroken masses" which Blake proclaims to be
the source of grandeur in art. The landscape background is indeed a masterpiece of beauty and repose;
the mysterious cool grey light of early morning is rendered exquisitely, and the mottled ranks of dark cirrhus
cloud which face the first rays of the rising sun witness
the intimacy of Blake's acquaintance with the Nature
he affected to despise. As for the cavalcade itself,
Blake's early study of Gothic sculpture had no doubt
fitted him to enter readily into the spirit of the time;
yet the delicacy of his perception, the completeness and
variety and appropriateness of the characterisation, the
rhythmic beauty of the grouping, all show the genius of
a master exercised upon material as exacting as any that
the art could offer him. The horses alone would suffice
to place the picture in the front rank of imaginative
work. It has been complained that they are wooden
and stiff-kneed. The answer is that they are thirteenth
century horses; their stiffness is a contribution to the
effect. As to the subtle suggestions of type and temperament by which they are related to their riders,
these are beyond praise. One of the most interesting
features of this work is the sustained and concentrated
employment of imaginative effort which it demanded.
We should have been prepared to find Blake running
riot, entering only here and there into the spirit of

Chaucer, for the most part expressing something as remote from his original as is his picture of *The Bard* from Gray. But the subject is in fact wholly congenial to him, and his original gift, far from being hampered by the illustrative function required of it, has hardly anywhere expressed itself more convincingly.

The *Illustrations to the Book of Job* offer a parallel instance of the same truth. There was, of course, far wider scope here for imaginative flights of the most daring kind, and Blake has not scrupled to avail himself of it. And yet the central quality of the series comes of his intimacy and familiarity with the theme. It was not to Blake a story into which he needed to enter by seeing through another's eyes; he saw through his own eyes, regarding Job's life as a prototype of his own. It is on this account—because Blake has, throughout the series, a secure footing on familiar soil—that his work is so little encumbered with lifeless extravagances. It was a part of his philosophic creed that each man's universe consisted simply of his own house and garden and the heavenly lights that he could see from it and that shone on him there. And so the sun and moon and morning star are in personal attendance upon Job, rising as he rises, sinking to the sound of his evening hymn, or blazing above his sacrifice, not because he is Job, but rather because he is, not Job, but Blake

P

himself.   It is worth noting in this connection that the
figure of Job's wife is treated throughout the series
with an unfaltering sympathy and devotion.   The
attitudes of the three friends degenerate more than once
into mere antics; Job's wife though often overwhelmed
is always dignified, and, in her dumb identification of
herself with her husband in his sufferings, there is more
of the beauty of true human feeling than Blake shows
in any other part of his work.

The designs to Thornton's *Pastorals*, four of which
are figured opposite, were executed in the year 1820,
and as an isolated effort in a quite unfamiliar
medium are of peculiar interest, suggesting the possibility of an inference as to the qualities Blake was most
anxious to secure.   Blake's history is a perpetual series
of paradoxes.   His natural leaning as a painter is
towards clear, pale, even tints, revealing form.   Of his
single series of wood-cuts, the most remarkable feature
would appear, without exception, to be the handling of
the effects of light ; and there is Ruskin's authority for
the assertion that the *Illustrations to the Book of Job*
number this same quality among their greatest.   " In
expressing conditions of glaring and flickering light
Blake is greater than Rembrandt."   Yet it may be
questioned whether in the woodcuts this was Blake's
deliberate intention.   Each of the four examples here

VERGIL ILLUSTRATED FOR SCHOOLBOYS
British Museum

To face p. 226

reproduced has, of course, an ostensible reference to some passage in the work he is illustrating:

> The damp cold greensward for my nightly bed
> And some slaunt willow's trunk to rest my head.

or,

> And now behold the sun's departing ray
> O'er yonder hill, the sign of ebbing day,
> With songs the jovial herds return from plow . . .

but, again, the poetical quality of the design is in very slight relation to its professed subject. Blake's delight has spent itself principally upon the vividness of contrast between pure white and pitchy black to which his medium lends itself; and whatever the object he depicts, be it a plough-handle, or a winding stream, or a mile-stone, or the full moon in eclipse, he will make it serve the purpose if he can. Whether the tortured tree and corn prostrate in the field behind it really convey the impression of a storm of wind, I never know. It is what the theme requires, and what the details of its treatment point to. But the whole design, with its sharp relief and mottled points of light, has, to my mind, the character of a lunar landscape, and it is, I think, really in the singularly direct revelation, given in this and all the other designs, of the artist's instinctive sympathy with his materials and his tool, partly adventitious, partly, as in the works of the primitives, dependent upon his very want of familiarity with them, that the chief charm of these woodcuts is to be found. The exhilaration of them is that they are entirely unmechanical. " Improvement," as Blake says, " makes straight roads, but crooked roads without improvement are the roads of genius." It is an irresistible instinct in art to treasure every symptom of the artist's living purpose ; the moment an artist becomes accomplished and skilled, there is a danger that he will allow paint or pen to run away with him. While he remains ignorant, he bends his mind to extract their full meaning from his materials, and his very errors become a source of delight. Here, undoubtedly, we have the reply which must be given to all those who, from the time when Blake's poetry first began to be appreciated, have aimed at rehabilitating his metres. Critics have been divided into two camps, the tendency on the one side being to assert that the faults are merely trivial, and such as any professor of poetics could rectify with his left hand ; on the other, that they are not faults at all. But both sides surely are mistaken. The fact is that the faults are not less faults because they cannot be corrected, not less faults because they are inseparably interwoven with the pattern of poems that are exquisite in spite of them, and which would fall to pieces if they were taken away.

Next to Blake's work as an engraver, it will be natural to pass in review the series of books of illuminated printing which are his most original and most representative contribution to art and literature. During the first years of his married life, his brother Robert, to whom he was particularly devoted, lived with him as an apprentice, and shared his artistic aspirations. After Robert's death the old partnership was maintained by his brother " in the realm of his imagination," and he always attributed to Robert the idea in which his, now famous, method of combined printing and engraving originated. Briefly, he drew his design and wrote his text on copper, using for ink a material impervious to acid; the plate was then plunged in a bath of acid, so that the unprotected parts were eaten away, leaving the text and design in bold relief. This method was first used by Blake for his *Songs of Innocence* in 1789, and he continued to use it with increasing mastery until his straitening circumstances put the materials he required for it out of his reach. The drudgery it entailed must have been immense. It is not surprising that Blake should have told Crabb Robinson he would " print no more." The marvel is that he should have printed as much as he did; and any who are inclined to mock at Blake for his overweaning self-assurance, may do well to remember that it spent itself for the most part in fortifying him in the pursuit of wholly unrequited labour. His original intention was to use the printed sheet merely as a basis for illumination; but the best of the designs had from the first a delicate artistic quality of their own, and are quite independent of colour for their effect. His last monumental work, the *Jerusalem*, shows page after page of printing and design, which—quite apart from their literary and artistic purpose—are, for mere boldness and beauty of handling, a delight to the eye. The two reproductions (pp. 26 and 159), taken from the copy of the book in the Print Room of the British Museum, give very little idea of the effect in the original, where they are printed, as Blake says, " on the most beautiful wove paper that could be procured," and are also of a considerably larger size. But some of the most interesting and characteristic traits appear with tolerable distinctness. There is, of course, neither dead white nor glossy black in the work as Blake left it, but everywhere a subdued and almost porous lustre, which consorts wonderfully with the apparent roughness of the outlines, and with the dazzling patches of uncouth darkness strewn over the page. Partly this, and still more the life and sensitiveness of these rough lines and the severe economy maintained by Blake in his use of them, constitute, from the point

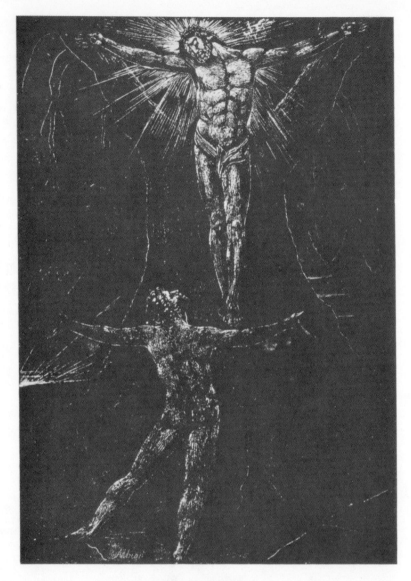

THE CRUCIFIXION
BRITISH MUSEUM

To face p. 231

of view of craftsmanship, the sterling merits of the work.   And nothing is more obvious here—spite of all the mystic meanings which lay siege to every nook and corner of the design—than that the pure artistic impulse is in the ascendant.   Los, Urizen, Jerusalem, and all the mystic cities, moods, and states are sorry portents indeed to the uninitiate; but Blake himself is so at home with them that he can put them through the performance of the strange long programme of their passions—we cannot question it—for sheer joy of seeing how they will look.   And it will be admitted that, for the most part, they look magnificent.   The *Crucifixion,* figured opposite, gives an effect so different that it appears at first sight almost incredible that this should have been obtained by the same method and with the same materials.   Such is, however, the case; and there are, indeed, a considerable number of plates, particularly in the *Milton,* where the design is similarly carried out. Instead of the design being drawn directly upon the plate and printed dark on light, the plate is blackened over, and the design left to assert itself, as in a woodcut, light against a background of darkness.   The effect, though not always very happily made use of, is in this instance superb.   Indeed, this drawing of the crucifixion, both in its conception and in its execution, is one of Blake's very noblest works.   He is not thinking primarily

of a historical event, and therefore combines with his
treatment of the subject accessories which to minds un-
acquainted with his individual mode of thought may
seem merely incidental.   The crucifixion he presents is
what he would call the eternal crucifixion, the crucifixion
that goes on daily wherever pride vanquishes love. Yet
the face and form of his Christ are such as only the
greatest artists, men to whom religion was, as to Blake
it was, the very core of life, have proved themselves
capable of realising.   The strength and tenderness that
Blake shows here, and in the hardly less noble plate with
which his *Jerusalem* comes to a close,[1] suffice to place
him, not indeed in his artistic achievement, but in the
beauty and rarity of his spiritual insight, by the side of
Giotto and Fra Angelico.

The method, which in these books Blake adopts,
of combining text and illustration in one decorative whole, gave him a remarkable opportunity for
the development of a faculty which must in any case
have been strong in him. Not the least interesting
reflection on his doctrine of liberty and expansion is
that he always shows himself greatest when working
under severely appointed and clearly recognisable restrictions.   Such restrictions are, of course, the very
hypothesis of all art, and a creative vehemency like

1 Figured on p. 55.

Blake's runs to waste the moment they are lost sight of.
Now, the mere presence of written words upon the page
cannot but act in itself as a continual jog to the mind,
and keep automatically before the artist certain necessary
limitations in the sphere within which he is at work.
It does nothing to check the irresistible flow of Blake's
idea, but adds, as it were, a rippling vibrancy to the
stream, and gives a sense of purpose, deliberation, fulfilment, to the course it follows.   And these are the very
qualities which the majority of Blake's subject-pictures
so conspicuously lack.   Thus it is to the borders of the
illuminated books that we must turn if we wish to find
a perfect treatment by Blake of the human figure, observing how in a space perhaps not half an inch across,
and with but two or three unhesitating strokes, he puts
not only a touch of exquisite embroidery upon his page,
but expresses all that he most deeply feels of life,
thought, and emotion.   What could be lovelier than the
little group of mother, baby, and angel, who, in accompaniment to the song of *Infant Joy*, meet within the
sheltering petals of a rose ?   What more august than
the prophetic figures relieved by background of storm
and billowy cloud, who herald the impassioned utterance
of the *America* ?   What is true of the human form is
true in a comparative degree of others also.   The
splendid serpent who luxuriates coil upon coil over the

frontispiece to the *Europe* is perfect because he perfectly enacts the decorative *rôle* required of him; and
he is all the better as a symbol of the infinite on that
account.   Under Blake's decorative genius the very
letters of the alphabet begin to breathe and live.   Thus
this peculiar combination of engraved text and design
provided him with the medium in which his most
cherished ideals fulfil themselves, and his most riotous
impulses are clothed spontaneously in ordered loveliness.
Page after page is a living, life-communicating mosaic
of natural or unnatural forms, poured out in reckless
redundance by an inexhaustible invention.   Taking up,
without being aware of it, the heaviest of fetters, forthwith Blake is free to discard all thought of fetters
more; he forgets that he is working in confinement,
remembers only that he may do what he will.

Coming to the colouring of these printed sheets, we
are brought face to face with one of the most perplexing
problems in Blake's work and attitude to his work.
When he first printed his *Songs oj Innocence and
Experience*, and undertook to supply the twenty-five
designs in colours for five shillings, what standard of
workmanship can we suppose him to have set himself?
Ought it to be a matter for surprise that the painting
is not as a rule a serious contribution to the art,
and that it is a point of convenience in criticism to

"THOUGHT FROZE THE INFINITE TO A SERPENT"
BRITISH MUSEUM

To face p. 234

speak of a great part of this work of illustration as executed by Blake's wife ? How much she actually helped
her husband is a problem not to be determined by
examination of the books ; when the workmanship is
abnormally careless, crude, or clumsy, Blake's character
is generally saved by the assumption that his wife is
responsible for it. But the fact that his handiwork
descends to the level of hers and that the two become
indistinguishable, shows how rough and rude his
method often must have been. It has to be admitted
that Blake's uncompromising idealism in art was only
maintained at the cost of an almost incredible blind-
ness. Some of his work—about which there is no
reason to suppose he was not as serious as about all the
rest—is so bad that it would do little credit to a school-
boy. There is a picture of *St. Paul and the Viper,* and
another of the *Pardon of Absalom,* in which every
figure is either mean or monstrous and the colouring
an act of cruelty ; and there are even one or two
pages in his engraved book *Milton* executed with the
same insulting recklessness. In this we see again the
seamy side of Blake's system of pure spontaneity. Being
sometimes genuinely unconscious of the difference between his bad work and his good, there grew up in him
a kind of perverseness which kept him from even the
healthier exercise of natural and necessary self-criticism.

It is only too likely that he believed all the hasty
tinting of his printed books to be immortal and inspired.   The truth is that much, one is almost tempted
to say the greater part, of it is a defacement of the
beautiful engraved text it is intended to adorn.   These
remarks are, of course, of no value except as a warning
to the enthusiast, and a vindication of Blake's true
renown.   It does not follow because a book bears
his name, and may even have been worked on by
his hand, that it has artistic significance or is,
in fact, anything better than a curio.   If so much be
conceded, we can proceed freely to assert that this
branch of Blake's activity includes some of the most
radiant and exhilarating of his effects, some of the most
unique and most impressive of his symphonies in colour.
He worked sometimes with transparent colours, sometimes with opaque, or with a mixture of the two ; in
the first case, trusting to the engraved outline to assert
itself and give precision to forms which were not always
too carefully followed by the brush ; in the second,
taking the print as a mere basis and constructing upon
it a phantasy which would continue to stimulate him as
he proceeded with the work, till it issued at last, not
only in an elaborate translation, but in a fundamental
restatement, of the original idea.   The first method
associates itself naturally with the *Songs of Innocence*

and the *Book of Thel;* needless to say, there is no hope
of giving any idea of it in a reproduction; and it may
be added that all the so-called facsimiles of Blake's
coloured books, while they succeed in perpetuating his
errors, invariably miss that indefinable purity of colour
or resiliency of line which makes the charm of the
originals. The graceful drawings of *Thel and the Lily
of the Valley* (p. 18) and of *Oothoon plucking the flower
of Leutha* (p. 190) are both coloured in this manner.
The reproduction (p. 100) of *Thel, the Clod of Clay,
and the Worm,* shows what a different effect is produced
by the more elaborate method. The suggestions in
this of almost tropical richness and languor are not
germane to the subject, though very beautiful in themselves; and there is no hint of them in examples for
which the more appropriate transparent medium is
employed. But of course Blake by no means confines
himself, in using his rainbow method, to bright, radiant
themes of fleeting sorrow or joy. He takes delight in
its effect upon the page for its own sake, and words so
stern as those of his *Milton* are to be read at the British
Museum through an ever varying haze of pale crimsons,
blues and yellows. This copy unfortunately is not on
the whole a good example of Blake's work: after a few
pages have been turned, the sense of beauty in the
colour combinations is lost in the monotony of their

repetition, and the carelessness of their execution becomes increasingly apparent. The idea of a book written, illustrated, printed and coloured by one man is so exhilarating that we are liable to give more praise to the work accomplished than the facts always warrant. The truth seems to be—what after all the very circumstances of the case necessitated—that it is only here and there that a page is wrought to the level of high artistic perfection or even of perfect suggestion, and very rarely indeed that a whole book is adequately illuminated from the first page to the last. Thus the copy of the *Songs of Innocence and Experience* in the Print Room is of small value for the study of Blake. If I had not had the privilege of seeing the Beckford copy, now in the possession of Mr. Methuen, I could have formed no idea of the brilliancy and tenderness, the daring violation of natural colouring, the exquisite substitution for it of imaginative harmony and truth, with which Blake was capable of clothing and intensifying these early simple themes. More than once, above a horizon line of deep indigo he paints an evening sky so lustrous, deep and burning as to create an altogether unique and ineffaceable impression: or again, in a mere fragment of space in the border of one of his designs, spreads an unfathomable depth of darkness, blotted with pale, striving stars. The charm of

the colouring seldom lies in any recognisable relation to
actuality.   At its best it is the charm of piquancy and
surprise, to find that in the hands of a master of harmony there is no object on earth that cannot be kindled
to the " pure gem-like flame." Of course the colour
scheme is often frankly symbolical, and, throughout
Blake's work as a colourist, symbolic suggestiveness is
never far to seek. He speaks in the *Marriage of
Heaven and Hell* of a jealous green which is like the
" green on a tyger's forehead " (the very alphabet must
be turned to symbolic uses) and ideas of similar nature
engross him when he colours his design to the Song.
The tiger is seen skulking past a cold blue tree-trunk
under a gamboge sky, an altogether lurid and fantastic
creature, greenish yellow in the lights, and indigo in the
shadows, patched with red.   His flank gleams like fire
against the chilly tree, and in this alone can we trace
any relation between the poem and the design. Blake's
tendency to lividness of colouring is often consciously
used by him to secure a contrasting background against
which the liquid colours of innocence may be set to
shine in their most tender brightness. An exquisite
example of this is his treatment of the lovely song called
Holy Thursday, where the main effect is given by a
peculiar tint of yellow used for illumination of the
words, this passing in the first few pairs of figures that

form the little procession of the children into an almost metallic green, thrown against pure sky-blue.

The two remarkable designs which face pp. 35 and 168 are from a copy of the *Song of Los* which, bound up with the prophetic book *America*, is to be seen in the so-called Large Room, annexed to the Reading Room at the British Museum.[1] Unhappily including not more than three or four designs, this book gives a more adequate idea of Blake's power as an illuminator than any other that is accessible to the public. Oberon and Titania, enthroned upon the Water Iris, speak for themselves even in the reproduction. The mysterious hill and river, dull stars, and blurred foreground leaves make up a world in which flowers are lanterns as a necessity of nature ; and if the curving petals reveal a king seated, or merge yieldingly to the soft figure of a sleeping queen, we do not so much as rub our eyes. Los with his hammer, kneeling above his material symbol the sun, is far less effective in reproduction. The shapelessness, the sponginess of texture which make his limbs and particularly his knees and thighs so repulsive in appearance, as if they were hardly more than an excrescence from the bulging polypus forms on which they rest, are redeemed in the original by a bold

[1] There is a copy of this book in the Print Room, but it is of comparatively little value.

and splendid orange glow suffusing the whole body and
brought to a climax in the flame-like jets of tawny-
coloured hair. " In Mr. B.'s Britons the blood is seen
to circulate in their limbs : he defies competition in
colouring." This figure of Los is certainly a glorious
feat and not less so is the effect of intense glowing
molten fire in the presentment of the sun immediately
below him. Blake was a passionate lover of the sun,
and a close observer even of the details of his pro-
cedure in this material world. It would be needless to
speak of it, had he not seemed himself to state the
contrary. " *You*," he remarked to Crabb Robinson,
"never saw the spiritual sun. I have. I saw him
on Primrose Hill. He said, Do you take me for the
Greek Apollo ? No, I said. *That* (pointing to the
sky) is the Greek Apollo. He is Satan." The sun,
however, was a symbol of Los, the poet prophet, and
Los stood for Blake himself. Whoever else Blake
lost sight of he never lost sight of the sun. The illustration on p. 192 (from Captain Stirling's copy of the
Jerusalem), besides its strength and beauty, exemplifies
to perfection the peculiar biting away of the horizon
line which occurs when the sun is dropping behind the
sea : but of course Blake uses the effect to his own
purpose and gives his sun a more than natural splendour of rotundity. The sun's ubiquity and the size

Q

which under imaginative treatment he is capable of assuming, are really among the most thrilling features of Blake's work.

It would be unpardonable to leave this department of Blake's activity without referring to the illustrations of the book of *Urizen*. These are in themselves, like the text of the book, among the most peculiar and most cryptic of his inventions. The book is concerned mainly with an incoherent rendering of Blake's idea of the material creation, as a prolonged agony of involution, a gradual crystallisation and imprisonment of the spirit. The human body is, throughout, the leading symbol of this, and the births of its various senses or organs represent the progressive stages of the creative process. It is not surprising that the designs, in which these things are presented to the eye, are always fantastic and sometimes monstrous. Blake is here guilty over and over again of his old confusion between the pictorial and poetical imagination. But in spite of a pronounced tendency to this kind of error, the designs to *Urizen* number some of his most surprising conquests; and there is peculiar facility for study of them in the Print Room, as many of the coloured pages are to be seen in duplicate in the so-called *Smaller Book of Designs*.[1]

1 The copy of the *Book of Urizen* in the Print Room is only a moderately good example of Blake's colouring; some pages, such as

Nothing is more interesting than to watch the diversity
of means Blake will employ to produce similar effects
or to observe how in one rendering he emphasises and
articulates traits which in another are totally obscured.
Thus the design on page 11 of the book, which represents *Urizen passing through the realm of Tharmas,*
will seem fine and expressive till compared with the
alternative version.   The idea to be conveyed is repeated
by Blake in his *Gates of Paradise.*   The soul, half
drowned in the confusion of mortal questionings, is
groping up towards light and freedom.

> Doubt self-jealous, wat'ry folly,
> Struggling through earth's melancholy.

In one example we have a pale green sea, and the
colour of the submerged form pale mauve, touched with
yellow in the lights and lilac in the shades; in the
other the sea is indigo lighted with dull green, and the
flesh, more sombre, is also more glowing and full of
life. The result is a depth of combined gloom and
transparency which puts fathom upon fathom of water
over our heads—a very masterpiece of imaginative
colouring.   And yet it must be noted that the greater

22 and 24, are definitely coarse in execution or vulgar in idea ; and
there is a great deal of hasty daubing all through the book.   But
pages 10, 18, 21, and 26 should be particularly noted for fine effects.

force of this version has wreaked itself upon the eyes and mouth of Urizen, which have an exaggerated air, and that the slight tilt of the head, so expressive in the other, is also missed. If this remarkable design represents Blake's conquest of the element of water, the illustration facing p. 30—also from the book of *Urizen*—represents his conquest of the element of air. Were it not that the curve of drapery behind the foot is a little over-formal we might say that figures had never been more exquisitely poised. They swim in air, they float like clouds upon the blue. Of course the air has too much of Blake's attention, the mortal frame too little ; but it is worth remarking that the mortal body as we know it is inalienably bound to earth, while these of Blake's are not.

The year 1795, which saw the end of Blake's first outburst of 'prophetic' designing, was marked by the production of a series of some dozen or more Colour-Prints, which both for their method of execution and for force and virility of conception are among the most remarkable of his works. It is a serious misfortune that there is no worthy example of these on view in any of our public galleries in England. The *Pity*, referred to in an earlier chapter, the *Elijah seated in the Chariot of Fire*, which Gilchrist rather feebly reproduces, the *Nebuchadnezzar* opposite, must suffice to

NEBUCHADNEZZAR

MESSRS. CARFAX

To face p. 244

give the reader some idea of the tensity to which Blake's mind was at this time strung. The *Nebuchadnezzar*, we must admit freely, shows clear evidence of over-strain.[1] The more remarkable is it that in such works as the *Hecate*, or the *God creating Adam*, Blake can launch himself upon flights of high imaginative daring — an unscathed Phaethon — without the least loss of composure and with no observable loss of control. The method of execution employed was doubtless suggested to Blake by analogy from his printed books, and indeed appears to have been first used by him for illumination of certain pages in these books themselves.[2] It required, as they did, an inverse drawing of the design to be prepared, which was then coloured and the design itself applied to it while the colour was still wet. There may have been some economy of labour in this device so far as Blake made use of it to colour the engraved pages of his books. But he pursued it further and adapted it to designs of which he never produced and perhaps never intended

---

[1] Here, as elsewhere, I must apologise to my readers for putting inferior examples of Blake's workmanship before them. Appreciation of his work has for long been confined to a small circle, and those who have been interested to bring it more widely before the public consider, with some justice, that they have a peculiar right in the matter of reproducing his masterpieces.

[2] The illustration page 35 exemplifies the process.

to produce more than one or two copies,[1] for the sake of a singularly rich and mysterious suggestiveness of tone produced naturally by the pressure of the moist surface upon the dry, and not imitable otherwise by any of the painter's artifices. As the two sheets are separated, they show the least trace of a tendency to stick together, with the result that the paint, uncertain which it is to adhere to, is not distributed evenly over the surface, but everywhere drawn up into minute spots and ridges, and these so exquisitely variable in disposition as to secure, with no more ado, a delightful sense of the infinite underlying and emancipating us from the tyranny of the monotonous, the very effect which artists must for the most part spend so much labour to obtain. The discovery and use of the method by Blake is of singular interest in connection with his theories as to the minute particularity of imaginative vision. He was an artist, and when he saw that a fine effect was to be compassed, he did not always stop to ask whether his theories allowed him the use of it or not; he used it. But the fact is that the effect, besides of course being of limited serviceableness, is essentially of the nature of a fluke. You are certain,

---

1 There are two copies of *The House of Death*, two of the *Hecate*, and two of the *Nebuchadnezzar*, in existence ; but I do not know that any of the other prints were repeated.

indeed, to get a mottled granulated surface, but exactly what will happen when you press one sheet to the other depends on subtleties in the material which are quite out of your power to control. Part of the charm of the result too depends upon this very fact, that the exercise of the defining mind has been excluded. The delight it gives is of a very subtle kind, and comes really more of nature than of art, as though the artist had called to his aid the influences which rib the sand or throw a ripple over the high clouds at sunset. And half the value of the method, as Blake employed it, was that it filled up vacant spaces in his work, left the imaginative conception in its main outline clear and undisturbed, and yet prevented the background however broad from seeming negligent or flat. Nothing is more obvious in a review of Blake's work as a whole than that his root difficulty is in the complete maturing of his conceptions. It seldom gives him trouble to strike out his central idea; but, for the rest, he is usually obliged either to fill in his spaces with merely formal echoes or excrescences, or is led to painful elaboration of incongruous detail. His hatred of the idea of vagueness left him, in the abstract, altogether blind to the virtue of suggestion; he made no allowance, in his theory, for the fact that expression has its negative as well as its positive side. Because the content of imaginative vision is articulate and precise, it does not follow that it can effectively be placed in a context where every detail is equally articulate and precise. The result of bringing one aspect of the real into clear focus will very likely be to leave other aspects blurred. Most of Blake's visions were essentially of that kind which depend for their fulness of expression on what the artist has been content to leave unexpressed. The imaginative sympathy of the spectator is roused to supply a missing context, of which, if it were actually before him, he would only see the incongruity. Blake's methods are often such that, to the normal observer, the incongruity is far more obvious than the idea. This, of course, is in part to be associated with his greatness. " You ought to know," he wrote not very graciously to Dr. Trusler, " that what is grand is necessarily obscure to weak men. That which can be made explicit to the idiot is not worth my care." But it is due, in the main, to a refusal on his part to recognise inherent limitations in his subject-matter. The world which he wished to render objective was a world which has on the whole been best revealed by the methods of impressionism, and Blake in much of his practice as well as in his theory was, one might almost say, a formalist. It is for this reason that the rough style of engraving

A DIVER
BRITISH MUSEUM

To face p. 248

"PROPHETIC" FIGURES

To face p. 249

used in the printed books, and brought to perfection
in the *Jerusalem*, and the rough wood-cuts lately
alluded to, show him at his best, while the hollow
precision of clean outline, which appears for example
in the engraved illustrations to Young's *Night Thoughts*,
brings out all his least tolerable weaknesses. With a
few rare and remarkable exceptions—all, I think, works
conceived in the Gothic spirit and thus in their nature
permitting an elaboration of fantastic detail—Blake is
most effective where his method gives him most scope
for suggestion, where the defined is definite because it
has a background of the undefinable. And these conditions were provided for him by his method of colour-
printing with singular success.

Before coming to Blake's finished drawings and easel
pictures, it will be natural to say something about his
sketches and what can be inferred from them of the
manner in which he went about his work. The general
impression left by his completed pictures that his gift
was essentially for extemporisation must not be allowed
to blind our eyes. Enough sketches are in existence to
show that Blake's conceptions by no means leapt always,
like Athene, in full panoply from his brain ; that he was
capable, under favourable circumstances, of recasting
them and even of developing crude ideas until they
could lay claim to artistic perfection. The masterly

Angel of the Last Judgment on the title-page to Blair's *Grave* is a noteworthy case in point, repeated as he is from an altogether inferior original in the illustrations to Young's *Night Thoughts*. The pencil drawing opposite, described by Blake's biographer, Tatham, as *First Thought of Cain*, is not less interesting, in its concentration on the leading motive of the design—a motive which seems already bordering upon excess of violence, but which was destined in the amazing, horrible, and yet majestic, tempera picture based upon it to be intensified with every conceivable elaboration of dismay. The illustration which faces the preceding page may also serve to show that Blake's prophetic figures and the complicated action sometimes required of them by their creator, though visionary, had their place also as problems in his mind. Upon a sketch now in the possession of Mr. W. Bateson Blake shows an exquisite naïveté of self-distrust. The theme is one of his favourites— Adam and Eve asleep with angels guarding them. Throwing off the idea " in the heat of his spirits " he recognises that one or two of the details have not come out quite true ; but he feels that the insight which enables him to detect this may not be lasting, so he writes : " N.B.—Remember to make the thigh of Eve to join better to the body and also to make her a little bigger and Adam less, to make a right foot

CAIN FLEEING FROM HIS PARENTS
BRITISH MUSEUM

To face p. 250

to the angels" (crossed out) "to make the hips of Adam less." Alas! those hips and thighs; it was something better than memory Blake needed for a right treatment of them. The same error appears markedly in the rough sketch for his *Spiritual Form of Nelson* and terribly mars his final version of *The Bard*, "Remember to make the thighs to join better to the body." Blake would have been well advised to write the words in letters of gold and to have hung them above his work-table.

Of all that have come under my notice, far the most interesting and most important instance of the progress and evolution of an artistic conception in Blake's mind is furnished by a couple of sketches and a colour-print in the Print-Room Collection, showing early versions of the famous *Pity*. The sketches are both in the reverse position, an interesting sidelight on Blake's methods in preparing for his colour-prints. But the important point to notice is his gradual spiritualisation of the idea. In one of the sketches (1874. 12. 12. 148) there is a crudity of realism in the delineation of the prostrate mother which, if necessary to the theme, would place it outside the range of pictorial treatment altogether, while the attitude of the rider is easy and graceful, as though it were a charming accomplishment, a mere incident of his ride, to catch the new-born child. In the second (1894. 6. 12. 12) it is the mother's presence which is reduced to an incident, her head laid back in exhaustion, her whole body in repose. The rider's attitude, on the contrary, is tense and strained, and the child throws back his arms in an impetuous, impulsive revelry of flight. The aim of the artist is to express effort, daring, and speed: to the latter end the design has been elongated considerably, to the former, the rider has taken on some recollections of the Michael Angelesque. In the coloured version a further transformation occurs. The figure of the mother is for the first time draped, and all the expression Blake requires from her is concentrated in her face, which is marked by a hollow, despairing appeal. The rider, draped likewise, has become shadowy, phantomlike, with dishevelled hair that streams upon the wind. And now again the arrival of the child is, as at first it was, a mere incident of the ride; but for a new reason. There is no longer any sense of an equestrian display. We take all that for granted. There is not even effort nor daring now. There is only the rush as of a supernatural hurricane, the lurid phantasy of an impossible event. This sequence of experimental sketches would suffice in itself to show that Blake had some real faculty for the development of his ideas, and

would seem to make it a matter for grave regret that
he did not give it a more regular employment. No
doubt the truth is that his use of the faculty was not
deliberate. He constantly, as in the painting of
different copies of his coloured books, went over work
previously executed ; but whether the process resulted
in an improvement or not depended, in part upon his
mood, in part upon the circumstances of the case. It
the subject was not deeply congenial to his mind, the
recasting of it would probably lose in spontaneity what
it gained in finish and elaboration—as in the two sets
of illustrations to *Paradise Lost.* He might, on the
other hand, be led astray by absorption in ideas that
were not essentially pictorial, and produce a com·
position—such as the famous *Death's Door* [1]—by
fetching two separately invented symbols from his
répertoire and setting them side by side or one above
the other. If, on the contrary, his recurrence to a
subject involved a recurrent appeal to his imagination,
he was capable, as in the *Illustrations to the Book of
Job*, of adding touch to touch with constantly cumulat-
ing effect. Or, finally, chance might engross him in

---

[1] The two figures combined in *Death's Door* were first used to
decorate two pages of a book which is second only to the *Jerusalem*
in the beauty of its printing, the splendour, mastery, freedom of its
execution and design—*America.*

an essentially pictorial problem, and he might thus be
led, by the unconscious attraction of his theme, to such
presentment and representment of it in his mind as
every great composer deliberately has recourse to : and
then, at each re-kindling, the imaginative fire would
burn more brightly and more and more dead or
extraneous matter would be purged away.

We come finally to a consideration of Blake's water-
colour drawings and frescoes, or tempera pictures.
These, the water-colours at least, are extremely numerous ; and his inspiration is here as variable, his workmanship as uneven as in any other section of his work.
The bulk of them were produced on commission for
Blake's friend and patron Mr. Butts, and changed
hands at a guinea a piece ; Mr. Butts on one
occasion ordered fifty. Perhaps more clearly, on
account of the absence of original ' prophetic ' designing, comes home to us, in a general review of this
section of Blake's work, the range and exaltation of his
imaginative experience. He appears principally as an
illustrator of the Bible, and, whatever be the faults of
his work, he never fails to convince us of the sincerity
of his vision ; his mind is always concentrated on the
central issue, on the divine, or deeper human, significance of the event he has chosen to depict. But,
besides the Bible, Chaucer, Spenser, Shakespeare, Dante,

JOSEPH ORDERING SIMEON TO BE BOUND

FITZWILLIAM MUSEUM, CAMBRIDGE

To face p. 255

Milton, Bunyan, Gray and Cowper provide him with
subjects more or less congenial to his mind, and are
witnesses to his intellectual vigour. The illustration
opposite, one of a series of three pictures of *Joseph and
his Brethren* now in the Fitzwilliam Museum in Cambridge, is among Blake's earliest efforts in this style
and is a sufficient indication of the artist's temper and
purpose. The weakness and crudity of the work are too
obvious to need remark. Its merit lies principally in
what it excludes. The painter is absorbed in the
human interest of his theme; his attitude—in every
particular save one—is identical with the attitude of
the primitives. He cares for nothing but the truth of
the situation as reflected in the feelings of those who
have their part in it; there is not, for example, the
least attempt to render the magnificence of Joseph's
state; the background, itself a mere screen behind
the figures, is laid out in tortuous lines echoing symbolically the human emotions of the scene. In all this
Blake allies himself with the untutored impulses of the
earliest masters of art. He is distinguished from them
in his self-consciousness, in the fact that his method is
prompted by a deliberate reaction. This may seem to
be a small matter, but it drives deep. Nothing is less
charming, for nothing is less simple, than an assumed
simplicity. Blake in his reflection of human life and

concentration on its central impulses is as simple as a child. But his artistic aims were complex in the extreme; and his ignorance of form or clumsiness in the representation of it are the ignorance and clumsiness not of innocence but of experience. Thus though he remains always in the deepest sense a primitive at heart, it is often when his method most nearly approaches the methods of the primitives that he comes closest to fatuousness in his results.

The accompanying illustration, which represents *The Three Maries at the Sepulchre*, may be studied in connection with these remarks: it is typical of a large class of Blake's designs, and belongs to the period of his maturity. All the appurtenances are bare and unrelieved; with the exception of the tiny group of spires under the hill, there is nothing to distract the eye. Blake's absorption in the religious motive seems at first sight as severe as Fra Angelico's, and the manner in which he has represented the tomb gives a reminder of Angelico that pervades everything else in the picture. But these staring Maries are not the spontaneous expression of mystic insight; they are the laboured experiments of a far too conscious imagination: and, though the angel is more intimately felt, he is too little an angel, too much a mixture of mannerisms, to bear comparison with the

THE THREE MARIES AT THE SEPULCHRE

THE COMPASSION OF PHARAOH'S DAUGHTER
W. GRAHAM ROBERTSON, ESQ.

To face p. 257

unalloyed simplicity of fourteenth-century painting. Blake in fact works by a theory, which of course he can only exemplify when he forgets it. We may pursue the same thought in a new aspect before the much more beautiful design figured opposite, known as *The Compassion of Pharaoh's Daughter.* It may be taken as characteristic of one, perhaps on the whole the least interesting, of Blake's styles—the pallid, slender style—at its best. Naturally, to Blake's mind, the centre of interest is the centre of emotional emphasis, the child and the child's mother and the princess; we get quite a whirlpool of curves converging upon the cradle, and all the subsidiary details are carefully related to this, by contrast. Yet it is when the emotional effect is most studied that the pictorial result is at once least credible and least pleasing. No child could take the attitude assigned to the little Moses; no head and shoulders could crane as those of Pharaoh's daughter do. For this we may be humbly thankful. Compassion moreover is not the feeling conveyed, but curiosity and surprise, as though the child were actually hidden among the bulrushes, which plainly he is not. This is not great imaginative work. The failure is not in the refusal to insist upon the conceal-ment—a triviality, the omission of which might be taken as a sign of greatness—but in the concentration

R

on an equally trivial spiritual motive, which, unless the baby is indeed concealed, becomes not only trivial but foolish. Blake was led to these excesses by his oft-stated belief that " exuberance is beauty," or that " beauty is expression," and so forth. His pictures over and over again belie him. The beauty and dignity of *The Compassion of Pharaoh's Daughter* is given to it by the deep-seated pyramids behind, by the stately quietude of the princess's attendants and the palm trunk lifting itself imperturbably between them, by the bending bulrush and the quiet water-lily, by everything in fact that Blake has not cared to torture out of its true form or to endow with extravagant or impossible sympathies.

It was one of the most distressing results of Blake's philosophical doctrine " everything is a man" that it gave him an ideal justification for his habit of treating natural forms as a mere means to the expression of human feeling. Everything in nature has its relations to one or another aspect of life and thought. And perhaps Blake's greatest faculty as an artist is the subtlety of perception which he is capable of bringing to these relations, and the perfection with which he sometimes works them out. To name a few of his greatest works—the wonderful fresco of *Winter*, which he designed for a chimney-piece in Cowper's house, or

the luxurious, cloying *Bathsheba,* or the lurid and
resplendent *Temptation of Eve*—is to be reminded in
almost every case of supreme examples of his power to
translate the language of the sky or the water, of trees,
or beasts, or flowers, into the language of the human
heart. The animal which has allied itself most closely
with human feeling is the animal which he most deeply
understands. The horse is for Blake essentially the
animal of passion (not in his mystic language, but in
his work), and he paints horses as sympathetically as he
paints flames. On the other hand, to review Blake's
work as a whole is to be overwhelmed and even somewhat disgusted by the fluency and incontinence with
which he pours out his perception of these analogies.
For exuberance is not beauty ; and a rapture of feeling
left to find its own objects by mere magnetism is sure to
overreach itself in the end. In art as elsewhere, if
speech is to be effective, it must be punctuated by
silence. The effort to maintain expression at all points
at its intensest pitch results in the destruction of all
intensity worthy the name. The forms of nature and
the mind of man are indeed at harmony, and this
harmony is expressed in all true art. But the artistic
value of the natural forms in their relation to the
human is that their significance is more widely diffused
and that their sympathies though real are incidental.

Thus they offer spontaneously the very breathing
spaces which art requires, by their tranquillity support-
ing its passion and making it intelligible and sane.

The illustrations facing pp. 146 and 279 are conceived
in a rather different vein. Both are fanciful in their
conception, if not in their theme. Both are marked
so strongly with Blake's mannerisms that many will
conclude that there is nothing but mannerism to be
found in them. Yet in both, and particularly in the
Hymn, there is a quality of restfulness which gives
them a true affinity with the examples of what is
greatest in art. The *Christ Baptising* is a good deal
the more complex in aim and consequently the more
uneven in achievement. The shadow of that conscious
simplicity which is called insipidity hovers over both.
In the *Christ Baptising* there are several passages—for
example, the curly-headed young man on the right and
the curly-headed boy on the extreme left—which are
only not insipid because positively silly. And yet a
diffused seriousness and a deep religious feeling are in
fact the most pronounced qualities in both these pictures, and their foibles are atoned for by a hundred
evidences of grace and delicacy and charm.

Blake's rendering of the *Judgment of Paris* overleaf
may be taken as exemplifying the best work he was
capable of when rendering (as quite frequently he sought

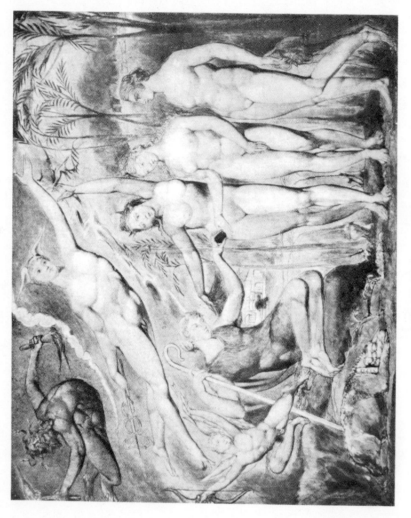

THE JUDGMENT OF PARIS

W. GRAHAM ROBERTSON, ESQ.

to render) subjects foreign to his experience and his taste. The forms of Hermes and of the three goddesses rank with the best of his nudes, and the whole picture is praised almost without qualification by well-known critics. Yet it is hardly possible to think seriously of it as an imaginative presentment of the theme: the arrows of destruction that descend from Hera's hand upon Troy are hardly more puerile than the stern denunciatory expression of the rejected Pallas, an expression which consorts with her nudity so ill. Then there is the dog; and the sheep behind the legs of the goddesses; and the lamentable effect given in the entire left half of the design by the fitting of each figure into the nooks and corners left vacant by the rest, as a child fits the counties together in a puzzle map. This last is among Blake's most distressing tricks of composition; and the whole picture, though it shows his accomplishments in an unusual degree, is singularly lacking in purpose and vitality. The office of Hermes, one may surmise, is to introduce the judge to the competitors, and this is what the wave of his left arm is intended to convey. It does not, however, really convey anything: and Hermes is in fact no more than a nude floating where he has no room to float. For all that, his ease and buoyancy are splendid, and if he were taken away there would be no picture left.

It is of little use to speak in any detail of works that are in private hands, and which cannot be put before the public even in reproduction. The bulk and the best of Blake's drawings and easel pictures are in this unhappy class. It is fortunate that the example of his so-called fresco painting, which, through the kindness of its owner, I am able to offer to my readers, contains passages of unusual power and beauty. The dark crinkled sea that stretches in front of the setting sun makes, with the bending figure of Job's wife just below it, one of the very loveliest products of Blake's hand and heart. The peculiar conglomeration of bat-like wings and sculptured cloud against which Satan throws himself, though lifeless, is characteristic. Blake had a number of stock contrivances of this kind which aped, while really superseding, imagination, and he availed himself of them far too readily. However, as it gathers towards the sun, the darkness and contour of the cloud assume a genuine menace of storm and are a fine contribution to the effect. The attitude of Job's hands, as well as the general exaggeration of his posture, is also characteristic in the extreme : and so is the disposition of the ground about him, which seems to be melting under the consternation of Satan's presence : at least Blake has contrived to give it all the appearance of swiftly flowing water. Is it possible

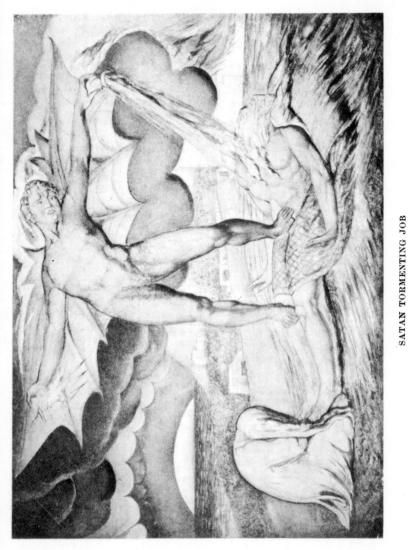

SATAN TORMENTING JOB

Sir Charles Dilke

this should be interpreted as the torrents of disease poured by Satan from his phial? Blake's literality of conception could quite easily have accommodated such an idea.

One of the most interesting features of Blake's tempera work is the variety of methods to which he adapted it. There are tempera pictures by him on canvas, on linen, on panel, on steel, and on copper. This variation was no doubt primarily experimental; but he threw himself with wonderful swiftness into the spirit of his materials, and, though often attempting what was impossible, yet produced now and then a triumph of felicity. The best illustration of my meaning that I can find is a tiny *Virgin and Child* which Blake painted on panel in the year 1825, the medium being tempera upon a gold ground. The picture had been varnished so unmercifully that, when exhibited by Messrs. Carfax at their Exhibition in 1906, it was almost invisible to the unpractised eye. Its richness of colour and depth of tone could not have been missed; yet the normal Blake lover passed over it as a work reserved for those who look for edification to peculiarities of technique. Under more careful scrutiny it turned out that the technical peculiarities had been subordinated to a religious purpose; and in fact that there was deep feeling in the picture, of which its peculiar scheme and method of colouring were essentially the vehicle. One noted first the exquisite delicacy with which the Virgin's halo gleamed against the deep blue starry night, and then caught the meaning of the gold-gleaming green of her head-dress. A moment more, and she seemed clothed in a harmonious sacred vesture of deep green and precious gold, that glowed, and at last burned, with the colour of the Passion behind the cumbrous heavily-serrated halo of the child upon her knee, a halo that symbolised the effort, more than the achievement, of holiness, and seemed to throw an almost scorching lustre upon the Virgin's face and hands. An equally remarkable instance of Blake's felicitous use of his material occurs in the beautiful and amazing *Temptation of Eve*, now the property of Captain Stirling and appropriately numbered 1 by Messrs. Carfax at their exhibition. This is painted on copper, and depends for its peculiar effect upon the lurid, lustrous splendour which it derives from the copper ground. Blake takes Eve at the moment of her triumph; her beauty is dazzling and resplendent, her arm raised in an ecstasy; she knows nothing of the vast coiling serpent whose head is raised above hers as if to take the apple from her uplifted hand. Yet the golden glow of her flesh is to signify that the snake has prompted her and that her triumph is his; and the landscape around them tells us that the triumph is a defeat. Was ever the depth and gloom of night more magnificently rendered than in this sky, where the moon hangs in eclipse? and what is the secret sympathy that unites the coiling tree trunk, the mournful waterfall in which the water has no strength to fall but seems to subside merely, and Adam prostrate and exhausted, sleeping? It is by his power to conceive and execute effects like this that Blake is numbered among masters of the art.

Blake is often distinguished from other artists as one who aimed at painting not the material, but the spiritual, world, whose eye was fixed not on visible, but invisible things. There is a certain obvious truth of intention in such a statement; but, as a means to accurate criticism or closer understanding, it is almost worse than valueless. Yet it is more the fault of Blake than of his followers if a confusion is made. He himself uses the term spiritual most ambiguously. In the National Gallery visitors endowed with patience and determination may discover a noble, deep-toned picture bearing Blake's name and the high-sounding title, *The Spiritual Form of Pitt guiding Behemoth*. Time has, alas! so grievously obscured the "lineaments" that it is almost impossible to make out what was intended to be conveyed. However, there is another picture of the

same kind in existence—*The Spiritual Form of Nelson
guiding Leviathan*—and in this Leviathan is clearly no
other than the great sea-serpent "drawn out with a
hook." Nelson, a nude figure in an attitude of effort-
less mastery, occupies the centre of the design, and
Leviathan's coils, with a dozen or more human forms in
their embrace, swing round him, as one might imagine
a whip-lash swung, in majestic servitude. For all that
Blake would have asseverated to the contrary, it is
obvious that what we have here is an allegory—rendered, indeed, with a splendid imaginative grip, yet
still an allegory—picturing the power of the sea over
man and of man over the sea. The name of Nelson is
taken as a type, to express in fewest possible letters the
kind of dominion Blake had in mind; and the " spiri-
tuality " of the form called his consists in the fact that
it might equally be the form of any great naval captain
—in other words, that it is not his at all. The same
is true of the picture of Pitt, except that in this case
the spiritualities are rather more confused. Blake
wanted to make a companion picture to the *Nelson*,
and Pitt in consequence had to be provided with
another big animal out of the book of Job. All this
is, no doubt, daring, impetuous, fiery, in a high degree,
but to think of it as a revelation of the invisible is a
mistake certain to issue in unhappy consequences. For

it is of the very essence of all art that it should have a spiritual purpose, and of course the art of painting can never, except by the most transparent rhetoric, be associated with what is hidden from the eye. The whole tendency of art is to break down the barrier which the normal mind sets up between matter and spirit, the senses and the soul. And indeed Blake's failure as an artist is that he attempts an impossible emancipation, and, by eliminating from the material framework elements that really are essential to it, produces, half his time, a result which, from the spiritual point of view, misses the force he intends to endow it with, and becomes merely flimsy. Cruelty, Holiness, Fear, and Love are all invisible. But it is not on that account that they are spiritual. The same is true of Time, Death, Conscience, the Church. And in so far as I make it my first aim to paint them, I am not more spiritually minded than other painters; it may be, on the contrary, that I am weaker in my intuition of the natural limitations of my art. The tendency of thought which led Blake to deny the existence of a material world led him also to attach a quite undue importance to certain mental processes which his philosophy was powerless to explain to him. He had a rather foolish horror of " generalisation "; he had a quite disastrous enthusiasm for abstractions, which are simply the same thing under another name. Blake once engaged in a passage of arms with Dr. Trusler which has its bearing on this issue. The doctor wanted a design to represent *Malevolence*, and Blake sent him something which he could not understand. " A father," Blake explains by letter, " taking leave of his wife and child, is watched by two fiends incarnate, with intention that when his back is turned they will murder the mother and her infant. If this is not Malevolence with a vengeance, I have never seen it on earth." The answer, of course, is that no one ever has seen pure malevolence, and that by resort to " fiends incarnate " the problem is evaded and the picture rendered meaningless. The mind refuses to allow monsters of this kind to be thrust into the heart of a human family. Their daggers and their grinning deformity fail to suggest any kind of recognisable intention, and the attempt to represent malevolence in abstraction issues in the representation of nothing, or of a mere nightmare at the best. This is the error into which Blake constantly sinks, and he involved himself in it by the pursuit of a certain kind of mental sublimation which he believed to possess a higher spiritual validity than that visible world which gives its material to the art of painting.

An artist, like all other men who use their mind,

depends for his success upon his power to neglect all those qualities in his business apparatus that have no bearing on the result he wants from them, and to concentrate his energies upon those that have. The power of invention is primarily the power to reject what is irrelevant, and works therefore with abstractions. The painter in dealing with the world about him abstracts (or should abstract) from it all qualities save those that make it beautiful and intelligible to the eye. There is no reason why what he paints shall be like anything we ever saw outside a picture, unless he makes it clear that he intended it to be so. He may paint the world flat if he pleases, provided he understands what he is about —that he is introducing a new abstraction into his art and entering upon a daring delicate adventure. More or less of abstraction there must always be, and its general aim in painting will hardly vary ; it will always seek to fasten upon the meaning or beauty which belongs to the appearances of things. Now the thinker (and with the thinker we may here combine the poet) makes other abstractions, having other purposes to follow. His traffic is in " ideas," and he quickly sets up connections between one thing and another, with which the appearance of those things has little or nothing to do. For most of his purposes, when he deals with objects of any kind, their appearance will be comparatively irrelevant. This truth applies so widely that one of the most far-reaching of his decisions, and one which he is very ready to arrive at, is that the essential nature of things is belied in their appearance, that one must distinguish between the appearance and the reality. We saw in an earlier chapter how, in Blake's idea, the world of the senses was a veil, hiding rather than revealing truth. Such ideas are familiar, and rightly so, in many kinds of minds, minds that is, whose central purpose is the pursuit of truth in a form to which the visible world and the visible objects contained in it do not provide a ready clue. A great part of the activity of thought is concerned with the apprehension of truths that have no immediately recognisable relation with anything that we can learn by the use of eyes or ears. This is particularly the case with truths such as those with which the mystical mind is conversant. The interest of the mystic is to trace out, and as far as possible to identify himself by sympathy with, the principle, the living principle as he believes it, by which all things are held together; he merely distracts himself and loses his thread of thought if he pays great attention to the shape and colour of this thing or of that. To pass from the underlying universal principle to its realisation in the particular colour or form would involve him in the unravelling of an immense chain of causes and consequences, for which his thought has not prepared him ; and, on the whole, his tendency is to snap the chain, and declare that the appearance is a delusion. But this he has no right to do ; if he allows himself to be deluded the fault lies at his own door. He has no right to say more than that there are many roads to truth, and that if, when you are on one, you take your bearings as if you were upon another, undoubtedly you will go astray. The road called art, and the road called mysticism, diverge widely, as we have already seen. It was the problem of Blake's life that he never realised the discrepancy between them. His aim was to make art —which traffics in truth as it may be traced in the appearance of things—a vehicle for the kind of truth which is not reached by considering appearances at all.

Yet he was not aiming at the unattainable. There are many roads to truth ; but the truth which all attain to is in the end the same. The painter sees what the mystic apprehends. And art, while it consents to follow its own method and to be guided by its proper laws, can shadow forth those mystical realities which we too readily pronounce to be invisible. That very truth, proclaimed by the mystic, of the living unity of all things makes this achievement possible. Blake is great because in an age of little faith he divined this possibility and demonstrated it. But the flaw in his theory which led him to rob art of its foundations led him also to regard art and mysticism as much more easily combinable than they are. Art cannot express the deepest and subtlest truths attainable to it by overlooking those that lie upon the surface and condition the attainment of the rest. It is only the painter who remains a painter that can reveal in his painting the world in which the mystic dwells. Blake produced many exquisite and some magnificent designs, and brought to the minds of all artists an aspect of their art to which they had given too little heed before. But his work on the whole is marred by the too easy substitution of the hieroglyphic method, of a mystical shorthand, for the true artistic presentment. He is among the great religious painters, the greatest our country has produced; yet the true, that is, the essentially artistic, significance of his pictures, even when they are worthiest of him, is often much more confined than he intended it to be. For all art is spiritual: all art is mystical. Whenever beauty is born, there is born something which to the artist's eyes is everywhere dimly discernible; and it is under this attribute that he worships the universal principle which the mystic recognises in its attributes of life and love.

CHAPTER XI

THE MYSTIC VISION

IN criticising Blake's theory of imagination I tried to
show that he had fallen victim to an elementary and
very serious error, by which he was at last led to deprive
his artistic impulse—in theory, at least—of the only
available media for its expression.   During the last
twenty years of his life he almost ceased to be a poet;
he remained an artist only because long years of unre-
mitting handicraft and unquestioning observation had
given him an inner universe of his own, and turned the
language of art into an unanalysed presupposition of all
his thinking, which no theory could shatter and no conviction undermine. But the error worked terrible havoc
even among his artistic activities; for he constantly
strives to give his art a quality which art cannot possess,
to introduce among its hieroglyphs the magic letter
which shall supersede them.   He would wipe out everything—the symbols and the world they symbolise—like
a child cleaning his slate, that, when he has made all

clean, he may write in transparent outline the one clear word of Truth. This instinct is Blake's fundamental instinct; and, although in the pure abstract form in which he pursues it, it is the denial of art, yet there is very little, whether in life or art, which, totally divorced from it, could retain its value. The instinct I speak of is that instinct which, when it is pursued alone, leads, as with Blake it led, to mysticism. The fountain of Blake's life was his religion. The problem which most deeply engrossed him, both as seer and thinker, was the ultimate problem of all philosophy, the relation of the individual human soul to God.

Among the last true poems Blake composed is an exquisite lyric which he sent in the early days of his sojourn at Felpham to Mr. Butts. Butts had written him a cordial, jocular epistle in not too perfect taste. Blake replied :

> To my friend Butts I write
> My first vision of light,
> On the yellow sands sitting.
> The sun was emitting
> His glorious beams
> From Heaven's high streams.
> Over sea, over land,
> My eyes did expand
> Into regions of air,
> Away from all care ;

Into regions of fire,
Remote from desire.

With hardly any loss of the buoyant ecstasy of
rhythm which is the charm of these opening lines, he
goes on to narrate how, with this rapture of light and
glory flooding him on every side, the world revealed
itself to him part by part in human form :

In particles bright,
The jewels of light
Distinct shone and clear.
Amaz'd and in fear
I each particle gazed,
Astonish'd, amazed ;
For each was a Man.

He is caught up into a trance-like detachment, and, as
if from far away, sees his home, his companions, himself
even, as the shapes and figures of a dream :

I stood at the streams
Of Heaven's bright beams,
And saw Felpham sweet
Beneath my bright feet,
In soft female charms ;
And in her fair arms
My shadow I knew,
And my wife's shadow too,

And my sister and friend.
We like infants descend
In our shadows on earth,
Like a weak mortal birth.

His spiritual experience is of such intensity that
human life itself grows pale before him in comparison
with it; and in its climax it is as strange as it is
beautiful.

My eyes, more and more,
Like a sea without shore,
Continue expanding,
The Heavens commanding;
Till the jewels of light,
Heavenly men beaming bright,
Appear'd as One Man,
Who complacent began
My limbs to enfold
In His beams of bright gold;
Like dross purg'd away
All my mire and my clay.
Soft consum'd in delight,
In His bosom sun-bright
I remain'd.

This, so far as my acquaintance goes, is the only piece
in which Blake, while attempting to give direct expression to a mystical experience, remains unquestion-
ably a poet. And part of the interest which attaches

to it is that, expressed thus in the true spirit of poetry, Blake's experience reveals itself as one into which all impressionable minds can enter, and to which, setting aside certain perhaps inessential peculiarities of embodiment, they will find much that is parallel in the annals of their inner life. Assuming this community in the experience, let us consider the peculiar form in which it came to Blake. Here we have a theme which there is a danger of handling too summarily. We may say, on the one side, that, like all visionaries, he saw what he had prepared himself to see; and that the content of his vision (as distinguished from the joy he had in it and his conviction of a truth revealed to him, both of which become real to us as we read) is singularly artificial and uninspiring. On the other hand, the very artificiality of his ideas, though coming— whence else could they come ?—from the mind-forged manacles of his previous habit of thought, came yet from one of the deepest veins of his thinking; and we shall be richly repaid if we can trace it home. With much else that became most individual in his philosophy, Blake owed these ideas to Swedenborg. " God is very man," writes Swedenborg in his *Angelic Wisdom*, " In all heavens there is no other idea of God than the idea of a man. The reason is that heaven, as a whole, and in every part, is in form as a man, and the Divine

which is with the angels constitutes heaven. . . . The
Africans, who acknowledge one God . . . entertain
concerning God the idea of a man. When they hear
that a number of persons entertain the idea of God as
of a little cloud in mid-air, they ask where such persons
are, and, having been told that they are among the
Christians, they declare it to be impossible :" to
which Blake adds a note : " Man can have no idea
of anything greater than man, as a cup cannot con-
tain more than its capaciousness. But God is a
man, not because he is so perceived by man, but
because he is the creator of man. Think of a white
cloud a sbeing holy, you cannot love it : but think
of a holy man within the cloud, love springs up
in your thought. For to think of holiness distinct
from man is impossible to the affections. Thought
alone can make monsters, but the affections cannot." The idea expressed in this is found already
in its simplest form in one of the most familiar
of the *Songs of Innocence*, that known as *The
Divine Image*.

> To Mercy, Pity, Peace, and Love
> All pray in their distress;
> And to these virtues of delight
> Return their thankfulness.

CHRIST BAPTISING

W. GRAHAM ROBERTSON, ESQ.

To face p. 279

For Mercy, Pity, Peace, and Love
  Is God, our Father dear,
And Mercy, Pity, Peace, and Love
  Is man, His child and care.

For Mercy has a human heart,
  Pity a human face,
And Love, the human form divine,
  And Peace, the human dress.

Then every man, of every clime,
  That prays in his distress,
Prays to the human form divine,
  Love, Mercy, Pity, Peace.

The idea of the " divine humanity " and its embodiment in " the human form divine " permeates the whole
of Blake's mystical philosophy, and leads him even to
an identification of the divine nature with the human.
" God only acts and is in existing beings, or men," he
writes on one occasion, and still more paradoxically
in that poetical challenge of his, *The Everlasting
Gospel*:

Thou art a Man: God is no more:
Thy own humanity learn to adore.

In other passages the mystical signification may be
seen merging into a more conscious symbolism, or even
sinking into that " totally distinct and inferior kind of

poetry " known as allegory or fable. Thus, describing
his *Vision of the Last Judgment*, Blake explains : " The
figures of Seth and his wife comprehend the Fathers
before the Flood and their generations; when seen
remote they appear as one man." Or again : " It
ought to be understood that the persons, Moses and
Abraham, are not here meant, but the states signified
by those names ; the individuals being representatives,
or visions, of those states, as they were revealed to
mortal man in the series of divine revelations, as they
are written in the Bible. These various states I have
seen in my imagination. When distant, they appear
as one man ; but as you approach, they appear
multitudes of nations. . . . I have seen, when at a
distance, multitudes of men in harmony appear like a
single infant, sometimes in the arms of a female. This
represented the Church." The startling expressions
Blake here makes use of have really very little significance. It is everywhere admitted that an artist,
wishing to give visible shape to an abstraction, finds no
form so widely serviceable as that of the human body.
What is interesting is that the disdain which in late
life Blake grew to associate with every kind of material
symbol, was never extended to the human figure : it
remained to the end an unconscious postulate of his
thought. And this was not only because he was an

"TO OPEN THE ETERNAL WORLDS"

Captain Archibald Stirling

To face p. 281

artist, though it is true that without it his artistic impulse must have altogether faded away. For him all other forms merged into this one; and the material world itself took on for him, in the moment of his rapture, the appearance of One Man.

A deep truth underlies the combination of poetry, mysticism and hybrid terminology, which culminates in this somewhat fantastic vision. The soul is dimly aware that its conscious life turns, as it were, about a centre; and that it can only go out into the world to lose itself and to find itself again there, because of a certain power or influence which comes to it neither from itself nor from anything it recognises in the world about it, but with which, nevertheless, it can come directly into touch by letting go its hold of everything external, by allowing all conscious operations of the mind to cease. Blake's great task, from which he never rested, was, as we saw,

> To open the eternal worlds : to open the immortal
> eyes
> Of man inwards : into the worlds of thought : into
> eternity
> Ever expanding in the bosom of God, the human
> imagination.

But in this he seems to be committed to the error upon which mysticism usually founders, the error, I mean, of

looking to the mystic experience as the source of a
determinate vision. The essence of the true mystical
process would seem to lie in a complete suspension of
our consciousness of finite things, a withdrawal of heart
and mind from all objects, all ideas, to which they may
be attached and perhaps attached mistakenly, a return
of the soul upon itself; not upon that self to which
experience has moulded it, but upon that other self,
that innocence, which is the condition of all experience;
which is the very principle of life and consciousness; by
which, if we but preserve it untainted at its source, we
enter upon a perpetual new birth and are numbered
among those little children to whom the kingdom of
heaven belongs. This suspension has the appearance
of a denial, and one of the errors of mystical practice is
to rest in it, as such; rightly conceived, it is only one
step in a process which aims at a wider, more perfect affirmation. The effort is to secure, as it were, a perfect
inward calm, to allow the troubled sea of consciousness
to subside, till it regains that fresh and pure reflective-
ness, which is not indeed in itself vision, but without
which no vision can be. It is not that an inward is
substituted for an outward eye; it is not that there is
any formal revelation made. In supposing this and
searching for a clear embodiment, the mystic is merely
reintroducing to his mind those limitations of the

finite consciousness from which his aim is to detach
himself. He wishes to be alone with the All, to be a
mirror upon which, while no image is to his consciousness reflected in it, there may be received, while he
himself remains unconscious, the form of the perfect
image of the whole. He has heard nothing, seen
nothing; but his seeing and hearing themselves have
changed their nature—or recovered it; and the things
he sees and hears are not the same. His eyes open
upon a new world.

To Blake the possibility of this experience was the
fact in which every other fact of life found its explanation. The Innocence, which was his secret, rested
fundamentally upon this. He knew of no Law and no
Morality which did not make the maintenance of this
kind of intimate spiritual communion its only test. As
I have said, he seems not to have understood his own
experience fully; yet he says so much about it and
reveals himself in it so clearly to his readers that we
are able, both from his sincerity and from his error, to
enter closely into the underlying truth.

In his *Descriptive Catalogue* Blake remarks that "the
history of all times and places is nothing else than im-
probabilities and impossibilities—what we should say
was impossible if we did not see it always before our
eyes." This is a truth which the philosopher how

remains in living touch with the deeper problems of
thought never can lose sight of. The existence of the
world, our life upon it, the growth of knowledge, all
these are things which we should say were impossible
did we not see them always before our eyes: but there,
before our eyes, they are ; the impossible has happened:
the human soul exists ; and so we proceed to inquire
what is the meaning of its existence, and what kind of
world this is in which its life is passed. Many profound thinkers maintain that the instinct which pre-
vails everywhere, even among the most primitive of
men, to think of conscious life as the centre of reality,
the instinct to believe that the world about them is a
living world, lies at the very root of all our thinking,
and points to a fact without which thought could not
go on. The process of knowledge, beyond acquisition
of new facts, consists in the discovery of order in what
at first seemed disorderly, and in the recognition that
there is only one system upon which the disorderly can
be reduced to order, and that this is for all minds the
same. With this discovery comes the conviction that
wherever there is the appearance of disorder such disorder is not actual, and points merely to a want of com-
prehension in the contemplating mind. Thus the ideal
of a universe, everywhere orderly and coherent, one vast
inclusive organism, enters the mind and can never after

be dislodged from it. And asking how it coheres, what
this coherence means, the mind has no response but in
the fundamental instinct just alluded to which asserts
that life, and that essence of life which on the one side
is power, and on the other consciousness, is the only
principle of coherence; and concludes that the universe
is one because it is spiritual, because it is alive. To
understand the mystical experience we must grant this
conclusion to be a true one. The fact, then, is that
the power which constitutes our life, and makes us
conscious of the world we live in, is the same power as
that which makes, or rather, is the world; and we, who
are parts of the world, are parts of It. Thus all the
diversity of things we see and know, ourselves the seers
and knowers among the rest, constitute one life together; every part is part of the living whole; in each
the spirit of the living whole resides ; and the condition
which makes knowledge possible to us is our kinship,
our identity, with this all-pervasive spirit; the fact, as
Blake would say, that we are members of the divine
body. This same fact is expressed by him in a variety
of ways. He attempts in the first place to formulate it
philosophically : it is, indeed, this that he intends in
his conception of the " Poetic Genius," a term that
occurs here and there in the *Marriage of Heaven and
Hell*, in certain prose jottings, and notably in a short

collection of some seven aphorisms entitled *There is no Natural Religion*. The first principle laid down is "that the Poetic Genius is the true man, and that the body or outward form of man is derived from the Poetic Genius. Likewise that the forms of all things are derived from their genius, which by the Ancients was called an Angel and Spirit and Demon." He clearly means his Poetic Genius to convey what in more familiar language would be conveyed by such a phrase as the Spirit of God; and his root idea is that all religion, the whole spiritual life of man, comes of the direct influence of that Spirit, working in him by inspiration from within, expressing itself therefore in a variety of forms according to the different weakness of different nations and individuals, but everywhere in its direction as well as in its origin the same—the bond of the brotherhood of the race. As all men, he says, are alike, though infinitely various, so are all religions, and all have one source. "The true man is the source, he being the Poetic Genius." In other words, the complete and perfect development in man of the seed of life that is in him would lift his life to a level with the Divine.

Blake's apprehension of this truth, so far as he apprehended it mystically, found its expression in the sustained emotional intensity of his life. "Man is love as God is love." The unity of things cannot be compre-

hended by human intellect, but it can be realised it
can be felt, when mind and heart set their questionings
and despondencies aside, and repose upon the assurance
that comes to them from within. And the action that
proceeds from such assurance is the spontaneous out-
flowing which in art is the creative impulse; in conduct,
is love. That, says Blake, is Life; is God; is Man;
call it what you will, it is the one ideal, the one reality.

The difficulty here, as everywhere, of criticising Blake
is that his words, over and above the conviction with
which he utters them, point consistently to an essential
truth. As we have seen, it is when he touches the
problems of spirit in its embodiment, the very questions
which should be naturally of most absorbing interest to
the artist-philosopher, that the limitations of his
understanding come to the fore. His belief that the
material universe was an illusion, that only the spiritual
world was real, was not in fact worked out intellectually;
he did not take the consequences of it. No artist could.
All material appearances would resolve themselves, he
believed, when the perfect insight of faith and love was
brought to bear upon them, into a uniform manifestation of the " Divine Humanity." And it was this idea
which he expressed in words that at first sight may seem
to have been intended merely for a parable; words such
as " everything is a man." Closer study leaves little

doubt that a parable was not what was intended. In his calmer moments Blake places the human form on a different footing from all others, regarding it as a final expression of spiritual life, and in his moments of ecstasy he finds all other material forms resolving into this.

> Each grain of sand,
> Every stone on the land,
> Each rock and each hill,
> Each fountain and rill,
> Each herb and each tree,
> Mountain, hill, earth, and sea,
> Cloud, meteor, and star,
> Are men seen afar.

This, to Blake's mind, was not allegory, it was vision. But, as vision, it was of course illusory. What Blake, like so many idealists, always failed to see was that to call the universe spiritual involves the acceptance of everything that it contains—from grain of sand, to tree, mountain and star—as being, each and all, just because they are parts of a spiritual whole, themselves spiritual; and that to set anything aside as material, to say "This is Satan, the work of the Devil, the death of Imagination," must lead, not to a deeper understanding of what the spirit is, but to a denial of the very truth which it is intended to affirm. If we thus narrow our conception of the sphere in which the spirit works, we do but leave great spaces vacant and waves of materialism surge in at once to fill them.

The ultimate expression of the unity of spiritual life, which Blake built up his great Babel-tower of mystic symbolism to affirm, is not to be looked for in any kind of system which the mind may artificially create. The only valid testimony is the living testimony of words or forms that do not affirm the universal divine, but here and there reveal it ; and to such we give the name not of mysticism but of poetry. The few short lines in which Blake says that God is in the lamb or asks if He is in the tiger have more meaning, more of true mysticism and true religion in them, than the whole bulk of his prophetic books. And the truth and the mystery are not summed up in their childlike trustful thought and sweet piety of language. Faith wins because there has been " vision," because the poet, child, and lamb are linked together by ties which are beyond proof or apology, and which, alike in question, or affirmation, or denial, assert themselves.

> Little Lamb, who made thee?
> Dost thou know who made thee ?
> Gave thee Life, and bid thee feed,
> By the stream and o'er the mead ;
> Gave thee clothing of delight,
> Softest clothing, woolly, bright ;

T

Gave thee such a tender voice,
Making all the vales rejoice?
    Little Lamb, who made thee?
    Dost thou know who made thee?

Little Lamb, I'll tell thee,
Little Lamb, I'll tell thee:
He is called by thy name,
For He calls Himself a Lamb.
He is meek, and He is mild;
He became a little child.
I a child, and thou a lamb,
We are called by His name.
    Little Lamb, God bless thee!
    Little Lamb, God bless thee!

INDEX

U